Practice Questions

1. When beginning a counseling relationship, you are ethically required to
    a. inform the patient of the limits of confidentiality
    b. explain that everything said in your sessions will remain confidential
    c. keep a detailed record of what is said during each session
    d. write very few details of what is said in your session

2. As you begin a counseling relationship, it is important to
    a. know if the patient is unaware of your counseling plan
    b. give the patient little or no choice in the direction of counseling as it could prove detrimental to the therapeutic process
    c. jointly decide, between patient and counselor, how the counseling process will proceed
    d. answer as few of the patient's questions as possible until the direction of the therapeutic process is naturally revealed during the initial hour

3. A client arrives for counseling with the presenting complaint of relationship difficulties. She goes on to describe that she has had multiple abortions, and seems to use abortion as a birth control method. You are personally opposed to abortion. How should your personal beliefs impact the therapeutic relationship?
    a. Your personal belief system will make it impossible for you to effectively counsel this client, and you should refer her elsewhere
    b. Your personal belief system should not have any bearing on the therapeutic relationship
    c. Your position on abortion will enhance the therapeutic relationship as it will make you more effective in teaching your client how to properly view abortion
    d. Your anti-abortion stance is best ignored and discounted while working with this client

4. You have been involved in a counseling relationship with a client for six months, when he presents you with a small gift. What should you do?
    a. Accept the gift and thank your client
    b. Decline the gift with an explanation of why it's inappropriate for you to accept it
    c. Request that the gift be given to you only once therapy is complete
    d. Accept or decline depending upon the circumstances

5. You are court-ordered to disclose confidential information about a client you are counseling. What do you do?
    a. Limit, as much as possible, any possibly damaging personal information
    b. Divulge any and all information about the client as court-ordered
    c. Obtain written permission from your client to share confidential information
    d. Both A and C

6. What should you do if your client requests to see his confidential file?
    a. Immediately give your client access to the file
    b. Explain to your client that such information is confidential and for the counselor's eyes only
    c. Accept or decline depending upon the circumstances
    d. Ignore the request

7. You are a counselor with several clients, and at the same time you are adjusting to a difficult divorce. You aren't sleeping or eating well, find you are highly distractible, and generally are less in-touch with your emotional state. You should
    a. continue to see your clients as you regularly would
    b. discontinue client contact until you have adjusted to your new life situation
    c. seek psychological help for yourself
    d. be alert to your mental status, and be able to determine if continuing with your clients poses any threat of being detrimental to the counseling process

8. A former client of yours has been arrested for a crime. As his former counselor, you are called to perform a forensic evaluation. What is your responsibility in this case?
    a. It is not considered ethical to perform a forensic evaluation on a current or past client, so you should decline
    b. You should perform the evaluation because you are particularly well-versed on the mental state of the individual in question
    c. You have a legal responsibility to comply with the request
    d. It doesn't matter if you perform the evaluation or not

9. You are the supervisor for a new counselor, and are asked to attend her wedding. Would it be ethical to do so?
    a. It would not be ethical to attend her wedding
    b. it would depend on your role in the festivities
    c. Yes, but only if you don't bring a gift
    d. Yes, you should be able to attend her wedding without a breach of ethics

10. While involved with a research study, you learn that several of your students are using confidential material in an unethical manner. You had no prior knowledge of this, and all of your safeguards for professional practice were appropriate. Are you, as the principal researcher, responsible for the student's behavior?
    a. No, if professional safeguards were in place, you are not responsible
    b. Yes, you are ultimately responsible
    c. Only the students who acted unethically are to be held responsible
    d. You would only be responsible if you had knowledge of what was occurring and did nothing to stop it

11. When publishing research, it is important to
    a. give credit to other contributors or sources
    b. not plagiarize
    c. submit material to only one journal at a time
    d. all of the above

12. When a conflict arises between the American Counseling Association (ACA) Code of Ethics and a governing authority, which takes precedence?
    a. Ethics always come first, regardless of the circumstances
    b. Ultimately, the law may be adhered to over the Code of Ethics
    c. Neither. The wishes of the client prevail
    d. There are no standards in place for this issue; it's left up to the individual

13. An ethics violation should NOT be reported when
    a. a counselor has been retained to review another counselor who is in question
    b. there is a personal relationship between the violator and the counselor who noted the violation
    c. confidentiality rights would be violated
    d. both A and C

14. What does multicultural/diversity counseling refer to?
    a. Counseling that recognizes diversity and approaches beneficial to specific groups
    b. Counseling that attempts to minimize the cultural aspects of particular groups
    c. An approach that all counselors should ethically be aware of
    d. Both A and C

15. Most ethical issues are related to
    a. an inappropriate relationship between counselor and client
    b. duty to warn
    c. confidentiality
    d. supervision issues

16. Only one psychoanalyst's developmental theory covers the entire lifespan. Who is he?
    a. Sigmund Freud
    b. Erik Erikson
    c. Jean Piaget
    d. Arnold Lazarus

17. The Id, Ego, and Superego are attributed to which psychoanalyst?
    a. Erik Erikson
    b. William Perry
    c. Sigmund Freud
    d. Alfred Binet

18. What is the fourth stage of Jean Piaget's four stages of cognitive development?
    a. Sensory Motor Stage
    b. Preoperational
    c. Concrete Operations
    d. Formal Operations

19. The term "identity crisis" originated with which theorist?
    a. Jean Piaget
    b. Sigmund Freud
    c. Erik Erikson
    d. Albert Watson

20. What is "positive psychology"?
    a. the study of the processes that contribute to optimal functioning
    b. a type of therapy that encourages positive thinking to overcome difficulties
    c. a discipline that analyzes developmental abnormalities
    d. a theory that eliminating negative behaviors leads to positive outcomes

21. If a client has a smoking habit, Sigmund Freud might say he is
    a. in need of behavioral therapy
    b. anal-retentive
    c. orally fixated
    d. in the latent period

22. Most mental health professionals believe
    a. in one developmental theory
    b. that no one theory of development completely explains the process
    c. that all developmental theories are, for the most part, inaccurate
    d. only in the more modern, newly formulated theories of development

23. What is John Bowlby best known for?
    a. psychosocial development theory
    b. behavioral therapy
    c. the Oedipus complex
    d. attachment theory

24. What are Lawrence Kohlberg's three levels of morality?
    a. Instinctual, Intellectual, and Physical
    b. Oral, Latency, and Genital
    c. Pre-conventional, Conventional, and Post-conventional
    d. Optional, Formulaic, and Oppositional

25. What is the female version of Freud's Oedipus complex?
    a. the Superego
    b. the Electra complex
    c. there isn't a female version
    d. the Id

26. Which researcher is known for his work with rhesus monkeys?
    a. Harry Harlow
    b. Sigmund Freud
    c. Jean Piaget
    d. Albert Bandura

27. What is Abraham Maslow's "Hierarchy of Needs"?
    a. a theory of personality
    b. a theory of human motivation
    c. a psychoanalytic theory
    d. a needs-based counseling concept

28. Down syndrome is caused by
    a. prenatal drug use
    b. environmental factors
    c. poor parenting
    d. a chromosomal abnormality

29. John Watson is probably best known for his
    a. Little Albert experiment
    b. contributions to psychoanalytic theory
    c. Bobo doll study
    d. intuitive learning research

30. Albert Bandura's best-know research was his
    a. psychoanalytic attachment study
    b. Little Albert experiment
    c. Bobo doll study
    d. behavioral contrast research

31. What did Lev Vygotsky stress in his developmental theory?
    a. six particular stages of development
    b. cultural context and language
    c. independent thought
    d. the conditioning of aggressive tendencies

32. Which one of these is a Freudian defense mechanism?
    a. anxiety
    b. repression
    c. superego
    d. nirvana principle

33. Which theorist conducted experiments regarding imprinting?
    a. Jean Piaget
    b. Albert Bandura
    c. Konrad Lorenz
    d. Sigmund Freud

34. Most counselors incorporate several therapeutic theories in their work. This would be what type of approach to counseling?
    a. psychoanalytic
    b. eclectic
    c. integrative
    d. cognitive

35. A patient arrives complaining of feeling restless. She describes mood swings and times of hopelessness followed by periods of high energy and creativity in which she can go for days without sleep. Based on what you know, what is her likely diagnosis?
    a. depressive disorder
    b. bipolar disorder
    c. ADHD
    d. OCD

36. A client presents with his wife both complaining that the patient has had a change in cognitive function including language and memory. The client denies loss of pleasure in normal activities and denies feeling sad. The client is able to manage his medications but requires someone to set up his medication box and set a timer for him. The worker suspects:
    a. Neurocognitive Disorder
    b. Delirium
    c. Depression
    d. Schizophrenia

37. _____ is a disorder of thought, unlike _____ which is a disorder of mood.
    a. Borderline; conduct disorder
    b. Conduct disorder; depression
    c. Bipolar disorder; schizophrenia
    d. Schizophrenia; bipolar disorder

38. Jeremy is a counselor. He believes in mirroring back his client's verbalizations, and not passing judgment on what they say. Jeremy considers himself a facilitator in assisting his client in reaching resolution of the presenting problems. What type of therapeutic theory is Jeremy working from?
    a. Freudian psychoanalysis
    b. Behavioral theory
    c. Rogerian, client-centered therapy
    d. Jung's client-guiding theory

39. Binge eating coupled with inappropriate methods of controlling one's weight may be a symptom of what disorder?
    a. Pica
    b. Anorexia nervosa
    c. Rumination disorder
    d. bulimia nervosa

40. A client presents with concerns about his health. He reports chronic intestinal difficulties, but has not sought medical treatment for his concerns. He says for at least the last five years he rarely feels at ease while at his job, and dislikes shopping or traveling (feeling his best when in the home setting). He is resistant to seeing a physician, but you find no negative ideation related to medical intervention. What might this client be suffering?
    a. general anxiety
    b. agoraphobia
    c. acute stress disorder
    d. post-traumatic stress disorder

41. A young woman comes into your office complaining of loss of appetite, nervousness (even when in a safe, relaxed setting), and recurrent nightmares of a past hospital experience from years prior, where she says she almost died. What might you suspect?
   a. substance abuse
   b. panic disorder
   c. schizophrenia
   d. PTSD

42. A single mother and a teenage son present for relationship problems. The son is actively defiant of instructions, argues regularly over minor requests, and can be spiteful and resentful over normal parenting efforts. School performance is marginal, but only one unexcused absence has occurred during the current school year, which is nearing its end. The most appropriate diagnosis would be:
   a. Oppositional defiant disorder
   b. Conduct disorder
   c. Intermittent explosive disorder
   d. Parent-child relational problem

43. A 40-year-old client presents with complaints regarding not feeling comfortable socially. He states that after gaining weight he now finds social situations to be overwhelming. He has stopped attending church and recreational activities, and does not engage in new activities, although before he was known for being adventurous. A likely diagnosis would be:
   a. Borderline personality disorder
   b. Avoidant personality disorder
   c. Schizotypal personality disorder
   d. Depressive disorder

44. Your client believes his favorite actress is in love with him, even though he has never met her. Substance abuse is not a factor, and your client appears to function well in life—holds a job, has social and personal involvements, and does not appear to be disoriented in any other way. What will you suspect?
   a. psychosis
   b. schizophrenia
   c. delusional disorder
   d. delirium

45. What is the cause of cyclothymia?
   a. prenatal drug use
   b. the cause is unknown
   c. child abuse
   d. chromosomal deficiencies

46. A husband and wife present for help with her substance use. She had been recreationally using cocaine on some weekends, and indicates that she has a strong desire to stop, but has been unsuccessful in stopping before. The precipitating incident was an episode of driving under the influence on a weeknight that resulted in her arrest, impounding of the family car, and considerable fines, charges, and increases in automobile insurance. This is the second driving incident in the last two years. The most appropriate diagnosis for the wife, given the relevant details would be:
    a. Stimulant intoxication
    b. Stimulant dependence
    c. Stimulant use disorder
    d. Stimulant use withdrawal

47. You are counseling with a client that voices complaints about significant chronic back and shoulder pain, which is the basis of a disability claim. During your timer interacting with the client you note that he is able to bend down to move and pick things up, and is able to reach over his head into an upper cabinet—all without apparent difficulty or complaints of pain. The most appropriate determination would be:
    a. Illness anxiety disorder
    b. Malingering
    c. Factitious disorder
    d. Somatic symptom disorder

48. The symptoms of schizophrenia can be categorized into three groups. What are they?
    a. Good, bad, and neutral
    b. evident, non-evident, and normal
    c. active, inactive, and edifying
    d. positive, negative, and disorganized

49. A couple presents for counseling. Evaluation reveals that the wife comes from a dysfunctional, neglectful, alcoholic home and has little trust or tolerance for relationships. Consequently, their marriage is marred by constant arguing and distrust, frequent demands that he leave, episodes of impulsive violence, alternating with brief periods of excessive over-valuation (stating that he is the "best thing that ever happened" to her, "too good" for her, et cetera. Which is the most likely diagnosis?
    a. Anti-social personality disorder
    b. Histrionic personality disorder
    c. Borderline personality disorder
    d. Narcissistic personality disorder

50. A patient diagnosed with depression and suicide ideation suddenly appears to feel better and think more clearly. His risk of suicide is now
    a. increased
    b. decreased
    c. the same
    d. no longer a risk at all

51. A 20-year-old male college student has been referred for evaluation by his family. They note that over the last six to seven months he has increasingly avoided contact and/or talking with family members and friends, that he often seems intensely preoccupied, and that his hygiene and grooming have become very poor. In speaking with him you note that he seems very guarded, that his affect is virtually expressionless, and that he resists talking. When you are able to coax him to speak, his speech is very tangential, disorganized, and even incoherent at times. He seems to be responding to internal stimuli (hallucinations and/or intrusive thoughts). The family and he deny substance abuse. Which would be the MOST likely diagnosis?
   a. Schizophrenia
   b. Somatization disorder
   c. Bipolar disorder
   d. Major depression with psychotic features

52. When a client's physical symptoms have a psychological cause it is referred to as
   a. conversion disorder
   b. hypochondria
   c. somatic schizophrenia
   d. Illness anxiety disorder

53. What does "appraisal" refer to?
   a. group testing
   b. individual testing
   c. clinical observation
   d. any of the above

54. What type of test is the National Counselor Examination (NCE)?
   a. objective
   b. projective
   c. subjective
   d. none of the above

55. The test created by David Wechsler is what type of test?
   a. IQ
   b. personality
   c. developmental
   d. none of the above

56. When administering tests to a client, the counselor should always
   a. educate the client as to how the tests were developed
   b. inform the client of the limitations of testing
   c. assure the client of the absolute accuracy of psychological testing
   d. keep as much information from the client as possible

57. What does "validity" in testing refer to?
    a. how sure you can be, before the test is taken, of what the outcome will be
    b. how many samples were used in evaluation of the test
    c. how consistent the test results are
    d. how accurate a test is

58. What does "reliability" in testing refer to?
    a. how sure you can be, before the test is taken, of what the outcome will be
    b. how accurate the test is
    c. how consistent the test results are
    d. how many samples were used in evaluation of the test

59. The only test you are using with your client has a reliability of .60, so you should
    a. feel confident that the results are accurate
    b. consider the results to be questionable, but still acceptable
    c. disregard the results of the test as the reliability is too low
    d. realize that the reliability is low, but still consider the test to be acceptable

60. What idea is Francis Galton known for?
    a. statistical relevance studies
    b. inherited intellectual abilities
    c. statistical validity studies
    d. personality testing

61. What is J. P. Guilford known for?
    a. the development of IQ testing for mental patients
    b. studies of inherited intellectual qualities
    c. individual differences and intellect
    d. intellectual testing of autistic children

62. Who developed the first intelligence test?
    a. Alfred Binet and Theophilus Simon
    b. Sigmund Freud
    c. David Wechsler
    d. Stanford University and Alfred Binet

63. What is the Rorschach also called?
    a. the random sample test
    b. the personality evaluation
    c. the inkblot test
    d. all of the above

64. Which test is one of the most researched tests in history?
    a. Rorschach
    b. MMPI
    c. MBTI
    d. Wechsler IQ

65. "Psychometrics" might also be called
    a. psychiatric interpretation
    b. psycho-monitoring
    c. psychological measurement
    d. a tool of psychoanalysis

66. What's the Myers-Briggs Type Indicator?
    a. a test for personality disorders
    b. a personality test
    c. an intelligence test
    d. a test of neurological function

67. You say a word to your client and he answers back with the first thing that comes to mind. What theorist developed the method you're using?
    a. Jean Piaget
    b. Alfred Adler
    c. Carl Jung
    d. Sigmund Freud

68. Your client is having difficulty deciding what career she would like to pursue. You give her a test that will help her make an informed choice. What type of test did you give her?
    a. an achievement test
    b. a psychoanalytic test
    c. an aptitude test
    d. a personality test

69. When did group counseling begin to be done more regularly?
    a. in the mid-1800s
    b. after the 1960s
    c. in the 1990s
    d. in the early 1900s

70. Which early theorist engaged in group therapy?
    a. Alfred Adler
    b. Carl Jung
    c. Sigmund Freud
    d. Carl Rogers

71. You have decided to organize a group therapy session that will be open only to patients suffering from depression, and will not allow new patients to join once the sessions have started. What type of group therapy are you offering?
    a. heterogeneous, closed group
    b. homogeneous, open group
    c. homogeneous, closed group
    d. heterogeneous, open group

72. What are some aspects of a "closed group" therapy session?
    a. stronger cohesiveness within the group
    b. less cost-effective
    c. allows for greater diversity among members
    d. both A and B

73. A common weakness in group therapy is
    a. not setting firm goals for the group
    b. having male and female co-leaders
    c. not noting problems in potential group members
    d. all of the above

74. Why did R. K. Conyne create the "Group Work Grid"?
    a. to address psychotic issues among group members
    b. to expand practical understanding of group work
    c. in hopes of eliminating intergroup resistance issues
    d. to clarify working relationships between group members

75. What is e-therapy?
    a. therapy that focuses on regularly spaced client evaluations
    b. online psychological treatment
    c. a new version of cognitive-emotive therapy
    d. a psychoanalytic treatment modality

76. You're concerned about how your group therapy sessions are progressing. What can you do?
    a. have an outside observer assess the group
    b. you can evaluate the group dynamics yourself
    c. ask your group members to each evaluate the group sessions
    d. choose a single group member to evaluate the group dynamics

77. When counseling young children in a group setting, it is helpful to enlist the involvement of
    a. parents
    b. siblings
    c. teachers
    d. pastoral professionals

78. In a group therapy setting, what is a "gate keeper"?
   a. a way to ensure that therapy goals are set and consistently met
   b. the individual who ensures the group remains "open" or "closed"
   c. a role assumed by a group therapy member
   d. the means by which therapy goals are safeguarded

79. Someone who always agrees with anything the other group therapy members say is
   a. nonassertive
   b. assertive
   c. passive aggressive
   d. play-acting

80. There are various stages in group therapy. Which of the following is one of them?
   a. sublimation
   b. invitation
   c. initiation
   d. storming

81. In a group therapy setting, what is a "blocker"?
   a. someone who blocks the others from taking up previous discussions
   b. a counselor who severely restricts group discussion
   c. a member who blocks others from veering off topic
   d. a group member who blocks new ideas

82. A client comes to you because her house recently burned down and her husband has left her. She is depressed, and expresses suicidal ideation. Which of the following would you consider?
   a. medication
   b. individual psychotherapy
   c. group therapy
   d. both A and B

83. What does "group process" refer to?
   a. the manner in which the group processes information
   b. analysis of the group's interactions
   c. the material that is being discussed within the group
   d. both B and C

84. What is "group content"?
   a. the manner in which the group processes information
   b. analysis of the group's interactions
   c. the material that is being discussed within the group
   d. both B and C

85. Most therapists consider the best size for group therapy to be between
    a. 2 and 4 members
    b. 10 and 15 members
    c. 6 and 8 members
    d. 3 and 10 members

86. What branch of psychology deals primarily with groups and social factors?
    a. Behavioral Psychology
    b. Cognitive-Behavioral Psychology
    c. Psychoanalytic Psychology
    d. Social Psychology

87. Who is considered the Father of Sociology?
    a. Sigmund Freud
    b. Alfred Adler
    c. Eric Berne
    d. Emile Durkheim

88. You are sent a client who is "culturally different" from yourself. Is it ethical for you to counsel this client?
    a. yes
    b. no
    c. it is only acceptable if the client agrees to avoid any culture-related discussion
    d. it depends upon how culturally different the client is from you

89. What is proxemics?
    a. the idea that proximity impacts psychosis
    b. the study of proximity
    c. the ability of one individual to act as proxy for another
    d. both A and B

90. An Asian client is most likely to choose a counselor who is
    a. black
    b. white
    c. Asian
    d. Hispanic

91. Your client feels his coworker's recent promotion was not because of the coworker's own merit, but simply because of company restructuring. He feels his own promotion, however, is a reflection of his own professional abilities. In social psychology/cognition, this might be called
    a. sour grapes
    b. transference
    c. attribution
    d. latent hostility

92. A cultural norm refers to
    a. how people are supposed to act
    b. how people act
    c. how people would ideally like to act
    d. all of the above

93. What did the Milgram experiment teach us about authority?
    a. people usually will not obey authority
    b. people usually will obey authority
    c. sometimes people will obey authority
    d. none of the above

94. Who developed the "social distance scale"?
    a. Eric Berne
    b. Avery Ellis
    c. Emory Bogardus
    d. Albert Bandura

95. What is the "foot-in-the-door" technique used for?
    a. compliance
    b. passivity
    c. aggression
    d. dominance

96. In a "self-fulfilling prophecy"
    a. the false becomes true
    b. what was true becomes false
    c. there is no change to the status
    d. both A and C

97. Which theory helps to explain prejudice?
    a. leadership contingency model
    b. Rubin scales
    c. catharsis
    d. social identity theory

98. Altruism may be explained by
    a. leadership contingency model
    b. social exchange theory
    c. catharsis
    d. matching hypothesis

99. Everyone says that Jack and Samantha are alike in every way, and it isn't long before they marry. What might explain their relationship?
    a. biological processes
    b. attribution theory
    c. consensual validation
    d. conformity

100. You cheat on your counselor exam, and you feel bad about it. You tell yourself it's OK because you'll be a great counselor someday and help many people. Your reasoning is an example of
    a. cognitive dissonance
    b. consensual validation
    c. social facilitation
    d. both A and B

101. The contingency model of leadership states that leadership is determined by
    a. personality
    b. popularity
    c. situation
    d. both A and C

102. According to the "bystander effect," you are ___ likely to help someone in need if you are the only other person present.
    a. more
    b. less
    c. just as
    d. none of these

103. Your client is struggling with a weight problem. She loves sweets, but she hates what they do to her body. Your client's conflict is one of
    a. avoidance/avoidance
    b. approach/avoidance
    c. frustration
    d. approach/approach

104. Acculturation takes place when
    a. two cultures mix
    b. a culture dies out
    c. when individuals seek to deny their culture
    d. both B and C

105. What does the Likert scale measure?
   a. attitudes
   b. feelings
   c. physical health
   d. both A and B

106. You are asked to speak to a group of Junior Rangers about future career choices, and plan your presentation based upon your knowledge of one of the members of the group. What type of reasoning are you employing?
   a. operant rationalization
   b. deductive reasoning
   c. inductive reasoning
   d. all of the above

107. You want to measure happiness, and decide that you will keep track of how many times your subjects laugh in the course of a day. You write down every detail of your study so it can be replicated, specifying the measurement of "smiles" as a way to determine happiness levels. What have you provided?
   a. a research report
   b. an operational definition
   c. a replication report
   d. an analogy

108. In a research study, every element of the population has an equal chance of being sampled. What type of "sampling" is this?
   a. random sampling
   b. systematic sampling
   c. stratified sampling
   d. none of the above

109. A study measuring the IQ levels of a group of men, of differing ages, performed on a single day is most likely an example of
   a. a cross-sectional study
   b. a longitudinal study
   c. a stratified sample study
   d. a systematic sample study

110. You decide to study how elementary school students behave in a classroom when adults are present as opposed to when there are no adults present. A few classes volunteer for your study, and you explain to them how this study may help to avoid future behavioral problems in the classroom. Which of the following are you likely to see?
   a. catharsis
   b. the Hawthorne effect
   c. the observer effect
   d. both B and C

111. You're assisting with a research study in which half of the subjects are given medication and the other half given sugar pills. Neither group knows which pills contain medication, yet many who receive the sugar pills repeatedly report positive effects from taking them. What would account for this?
   a. transference
   b. the placebo effect
   c. the Hawthorne effect
   d. research bias

112. A seventeen-year-old client has been referred to you for intellectual testing. What test are you likely to perform?
   a. WAIS-IV
   b. WISC-R
   c. WPPSI
   d. Rorschach

113. A parent brings her eight-year-old son to you, complaining that his teachers feel he is impaired. What testing would you likely suggest?
   a. WPPSI
   b. Rorschach
   c. WAIS-IV
   d. WISC-R

114. What does a frequency distribution do?
   a. It shows the distribution of an audio frequency pitch.
   b. It shows the number of times a particular value occurs.
   c. It monitors the ongoing results of a research study.
   d. both A and B

115. Your patient achieves a full scale IQ of 100 on the WAIS-IV. What intellectual level does this put him at?
   a. borderline
   b. superior
   c. average
   d. high average

116. You're asked to evaluate a client for possible intellectual disabilities. The client achieves a score of 50 on the WAIS-IV. According to the DSM, what range does this place her in?
   a. moderate to severe intellectual disabilities
   b. mild to moderate intellectual disabilities
   c. mild to profound intellectual disabilities
   d. severe to profound intellectual disabilities

117. In an experiment, what is the "independent variable"?
    a. the experimental factor
    b. the element that changed or manipulated
    c. the variable that depends upon what happens to the experimental subjects
    d. both A and B

118. What does a "correlation strategy" measure?
    a. how strong the relation is between things
    b. the way in which the experiment is conducted
    c. the "strategy" for graphing the experiment's results
    d. none of the above

119. A scatter plot depicts
    a. a multitude of single scores
    b. pairs of scores
    c. one score
    d. the unscored results of an experiment

120. A correlation coefficient shows
    a. how strong the relationship between two variables is
    b. the direction of two variables' relationship
    c. the degree of relationship between two variables
    d. all of the above

121. If there is a 95% chance that an experiment's results are not due to chance, one might say that the experiment
    a. has achieved reliability and validity
    b. would create a great scatter plot
    c. has a high correlation coefficient
    d. is statistically significant

122. What does the glass ceiling refer to?
    a. limitations in the workplace
    b. a developmental milestone theorized by Freud
    c. Adler's theory of passive resistance
    d. a behavioral treatment for phobias

123. Modern-day careers are viewed more as ___ than as a means to earn money.
    a. self-expression
    b. a status symbol
    c. a social expectation
    d. all of the above

124. What is "leisure time"?
    a. time away from work
    b. a term coined by Carl Jung
    c. a time-management tool
    d. a critical factor in Alfred Adler's developmental theory

125. Krumboltz's Learning Theory of Career Counseling (LTCC) is based on what early theorist?
    a. Freud
    b. Bandura
    c. Jung
    d. Skinner

126. The Theory of Work Adjustment (TWA) focuses on work in relation to the individual's
    a. environment
    b. psyche
    c. emotional development
    d. phobias

127. What does vocational psychology focus on?
    a. personality traits
    b. vocation
    c. psychotic symptoms
    d. both A and B

128. Two clients are referred to you and deemed to be "workaholics." One enjoys his work, and the other does not. Which is likely to be more problematic?
    a. the client who enjoys his work
    b. the client who does not enjoy his work
    c. neither is likely to be problematic
    d. both are likely to be equally problematic

129. Telecommuting often involves
    a. flexible schedules
    b. the Internet
    c. computers
    d. all of the above

130. Your client's employer has mandated that she take an immediate vacation. She is resistant, feeling she needs to work harder to prove herself. The company's concern, however, may more likely be related to
    a. cost-cutting techniques
    b. the eventual elimination of her job
    c. occupational stress
    d. none of the above

131. According to John Holland's six personality types, your client falls into the "realistic" personality type. Which of the following careers would he perhaps be well suited for?
    a. carpenter
    b. doctor
    c. artist
    d. counselor

132. The Minnesota Importance Questionnaire can be used with
    a. males only
    b. males or females
    c. groups only
    d. individuals only

133. What is the Minnesota Job Description Questionnaire used for?
    a. determining what job is best in Minnesota
    b. describing the characteristics of jobs currently available
    c. measuring the reinforcer characteristics of an occupation
    d. none of the above

134. In "rater bias," a supervisor who rates an employee negatively overall simply because of one very negative attribute is using what type of rater bias?
    a. halo
    b. severity
    c. horns
    d. recency

135. Your client has been out of the workforce for ten years while caring for small children. She would generally be considered a
    a. good candidate for employment
    b. displaced homemaker
    c. versatile employee
    d. none of the above

136. What is outsourcing?
    a. when outside sources are brought within the company to do a job
    b. when jobs are contracted outside the company
    c. using outside supervision within a company
    d. an Internet-driven management model

137. Your client repeatedly justifies destructive behaviors with excuses that attempt to depict them as beneficial. What Freudian defense mechanism is he making use of?
    a. rationalization
    b. depression
    c. reaction formation
    d. sublimation

138. What is empathy?
    a. a type of projection
    b. a way to experience the world as your client does
    c. a way to feel what you would feel in your client's situation
    d. feeling the same feelings your client has

139. What are some common criticisms of Rogerian therapy?
    a. it doesn't take developmental stages into account
    b. it assumes that people are basically good and healthy
    c. it may be inappropriate for some type of mental illness
    d. all of the above

140. Why does Carl Rogers use the term "client" instead of "patient"?
    a. to remove the hierarchical element between client and therapist
    b. to differentiate his type of therapy from psychoanalytic
    c. to promote a more business-like image
    d. for no particular reason

141. A focus on confronting clients and pushing them to choose the present instead of allowing the past to affect them is
    a. person-centered therapy
    b. classical conditioning
    c. self-efficacy
    d. Gestalt therapy

142. Your client shares with you her ongoing state of conflict with her brother. You encourage her to act out her thoughts and feelings as if you, her counselor, were actually her brother. What type of therapeutic theory are you using?
    a. classical conditioning
    b. Rogerian
    c. Gestalt
    d. aversive conditioning

143. In cognitive-behavioral therapy, behaviors are specifically related to
    a. early childhood trauma
    b. thoughts and feelings
    c. conditioning
    d. reinforcement

144. Your depressed client continually refers to thoughts of being inferior and unworthy of love, and chooses self-destructive behavior as a result. You believe that changing her thought process will alter or eliminate her depression. What type of therapy are you utilizing?
    a. operant conditioning
    b. psychoanalysis
    c. rational-emotive therapy (RET)
    d. aversive conditioning

145. Which of the following is sometimes called "third force psychology"?
    a. psychoanalytic
    b. humanistic
    c. behaviorism
    d. cognitive

146. With which type of therapist would a rapport be established the quickest?
    a. Rogerian therapist
    b. Gestalt therapist
    c. Freudian therapist
    d. rational-emotive therapist

147. What type of theory includes "reflection"?
    a. humanistic
    b. behavioral
    c. psychoanalytic
    d. Gestalt

148. You use a combination of deep relaxation and repeated exposure to help a client overcome her fear of spiders. What type of therapy are you using?
    a. systematic desensitization
    b. classical conditioning
    c. operant conditioning
    d. both A and C

149. Your client has a drinking problem so you start him on medication that induces nausea whenever he drinks alcoholic beverages. What type of therapy are you using?
    a. rational-emotive therapy
    b. operant conditioning
    c. systematic desensitization
    d. aversive conditioning

150. Giving a negative consequence every time an unwanted behavior occurs could be considered
    a. behavioral therapy
    b. operant conditioning
    c. punishment
    d. all of the above

151. Giving a positive consequence every time a desired behavior is engaged in could be considered
    a. negative reinforcement
    b. positive reinforcement
    c. aversive conditioning
    d. extinction

152. Who developed transactional analysis (TA) and "life scripts"?
    a. Sigmund Freud
    b. Eric Berne
    c. Eric Erikson
    d. Alfred Adler

153. One of Meichenbaum's three stages of "stress inoculation" focuses on
    a. the relationship between the client and meaningful work
    b. mastering the hierarchy of needs
    c. skills acquisition
    d. the relationship between the client and their family

154. You assign your client reading to do outside of the therapy sessions. What type of therapy are you probably using?
    a. busy work
    b. behavioral therapy
    c. bibliotherapy
    d. cognitive-emotive therapy

155. Believing that the significant other of an individual must love them for anything they do, would be an example from what theory?
    a. REBT
    b. psychoanalytic theory
    c. aversive therapy
    d. operant conditioning

156. Which is one of Glasser's five fundamental needs from Choice Theory?
    a. freedom
    b. wealth
    c. happiness
    d. meaningful work

157. If you believe that the only behavior you can control is your own, and that "all we do is behave," you may be an advocate of which theorist?
    a. B. F. Skinner
    b. Albert Ellis
    c. Sigmund Freud
    d. William Glasser

158. Many counselors and clients, in the therapeutic setting, would say that __ is very difficult to deal with.
    a. silence
    b. catharsis
    c. role reversal
    d. ambivalence

159. In Albert Bandura's cognitive behavioral therapeutic approach, ___is very important in developing adaptive behavior.
    a. aversive conditioning
    b. catharsis
    c. a token economy
    d. self-efficacy

160. What is abnormal behavior?
    a. behavior that is maladaptive and harmful
    b. behavior that is atypical
    c. behavior that is not "normal"
    d. behavior that is different from that of the individual's peer group

161. In psychoanalytic theory, a dream's "manifest content" is
    a. its conscious material
    b. its unconscious material
    c. its interpretation
    d. its real-life application

162. What is a "token economy"?
    a. a behavioral modification technique
    b. a temporary, experimental economic system
    c. a way to test a societal economic construct
    d. a new type of dream analysis

163. Your client wants to understand why she continues to bite her nails. You ask her questions to determine her thoughts before, after, and during her episodes of nail-biting. What type of therapy are you likely to be utilizing?
    a. psychoanalytic
    b. behavioral
    c. cognitive
    d. transcendental

164. Logotherapy focuses on
    a. pleasure
    b. power
    c. human will
    d. pain

165. As a new counselor, you find that you continually receive answers of "yes" or "no" from your clients. What might help to get your client talking?
    a. ask more open-ended questions
    b. make use of silence
    c. adopt a Rogerian-like technique
    d. all of the above

166. B.F. Skinner believed that punishment was
    a. a very effective technique in behavior modification
    b. not a very effective technique in behavior modification
    c. not the best choice for use in behavior modification
    d. both B and C

167. Your teen client (who is usually quite slovenly), tells you that he's willing to shower, comb his hair, and dress well on Friday nights because it gains him the attention of a girl he likes. What operant conditioning principle is at work here?
    a. self-instructional principle
    b. token economy principle
    c. Premack principle
    d. self-efficacy principle

168. If your client is taking a "tricyclic" medication. What type of drug is this?
    a. antipsychotic
    b. antidepressant
    c. antianxiety
    d. none of the above

169. ECT is
    a. incredibly painful
    b. involves little discomfort
    c. mostly used for schizophrenia
    d. usually administered for bipolar patients

170. Psychosurgery is usually considered
    a. a last resort treatment
    b. highly effective for many mental disorders
    c. too recently developed to be reliable
    d. a good choice as a treatment for schizophrenia

171. Which of the following is a general adaptation syndrome (GAS) stage?
    a. relaxation
    b. adaptation
    c. stress
    d. resistance

172. Emotion-focused coping is
    a. usually the best coping strategy
    b. less effective overall than problem-focused coping
    c. sometimes a good coping strategy
    d. both B and C

173. Your client is instructed in cognitive methods to reduce his high blood pressure. What treatment is he probably utilizing?
    a. transference
    b. biofeedback
    c. imagery therapy
    d. none of the above

174. According to Masters and Johnson, the human sexual response consists of how many phases?
    a. two
    b. six
    c. three
    d. four

175. The Yerkes-Dodson law states that people perform better
    a. under high levels of arousal
    b. under low levels of arousal
    c. under moderate levels of arousal
    d. none of the above

176. The James-Lange theory of arousal and emotion says that
    a. a physiological response precedes emotion
    b. emotion precedes a physiological response
    c. emotion and physiological response occur together
    d. physiological response and emotion are not related

177. Who theorized about "primary narcissism"?
    a. Jung
    b. Freud
    c. Adler
    d. Rogers

178. What would Erich Fromm have said about religion?
    a. It may inhibit healthy growth and development.
    b. It may be used to encourage warfare.
    c. It's fine to have religious faith and experience.
    d. All of the above.

179. Harry Stack Sullivan theorized about "euphoria" and
    a. tension
    b. stress
    c. loss
    d. abandonment

180. Erik Erikson believed that the "unconscious" was among which theorist's greatest accomplishments?
    a. Sigmund Freud
    b. Alfred Adler
    c. Gordon Allport
    d. George Kelly

181. Which theorist is well known for his work with prejudice?
    a. Allport
    b. Skinner
    c. Jung
    d. Freud

182. The key to George Kelly's personality theory is the idea of one "fundamental postulate" and eleven ___ that are designed to clarify an individual's personal constructs.
    a. corollaries
    b. ideas
    c. adjunct elements
    d. possibilities

183. Raymond Cattell's "factor analysis" theory refers to three types of traits. What are they?
    a. source, surface, and unique
    b. original, modulating, and final
    c. new, old, and resolved
    d. complex, simple, and modulated

184. Your client is taking diazepam (Valium). What type of medication is this?
    a. antischizophrenic
    b. antipsychotic
    c. antidepressant
    d. antianxiety

185. If your client is taking Thorazine, he's taking an
    a. antidepressant
    b. antipsychotic
    c. antidepressant
    d. none of the above

186. What would be the best description of hypnosis from the following choices?
    a. a drug-induced mental state
    b. a deep state of relaxation
    c. a meditative state
    d. a magician's trick

187. Hypnotherapy is used today for
    a. headaches
    b. childbirth
    c. chronic pain
    d. all of the above

188. ___ men suffer from depression, and most are ___ likely to seek help for it.
    a. Many, very
    b. Many, not
    c. Few, very
    d. Few, not

189. What does B.F. Skinner's "Skinner box" measure?
    a. psychosocial adjustment
    b. contingencies of reinforcement
    c. interpersonal adjustment
    d. animal magnetism

190. B.F. Skinner found that deprivation will ___ the probability of an operant.
   a. decrease
   b. increase
   c. not affect
   d. sporadically alter

191. B.F. Skinner would say that religion is
   a. an example of behavioral control through conditioning
   b. an exception to the behavioral rule
   c. a means of mind control
   d. none of the above

192. According to Albert Bandura, observational learning happens primarily through
   a. reinforcement
   b. trial and error
   c. cognition
   d. conditioning

193. One of the most criticized aspects of Sigmund Freud's theories is his view of
   a. defense mechanisms
   b. dream interpretation
   c. personality development
   d. female sexuality

194. Carl Jung believed that teleology must be considered in understanding personality. What does teleology refer to?
   a. goals
   b. the past
   c. the present
   d. early childhood development

195. Carl Jung's "personal unconscious"
   a. is formed at birth
   b. develops in later, more mature years
   c. occurs in the sensorimotor stage
   d. forms in the oral stage

196. The purpose of free association in psychoanalysis is
   a. to bring conscious material into the unconscious
   b. to bring unconscious material into the conscious
   c. to allow for a break from the stress of analysis
   d. none of the above

197. What is regression?
    a. a Freudian concept
    b. a defense mechanism
    c. a psychoanalytic concept
    d. all of the above

198. According to Freudian theory, where does the conscience reside?
    a. Superego
    b. Ego
    c. Id
    d. Preconscious

199. Your client insists that she is through with her previous boyfriend, but during a discussion of her current relationship, inadvertently calls her new boyfriend by her previous boyfriend's name. What might this be referred to as?
    a. a latent moralism
    b. a slip of the tongue
    c. a Freudian slip
    d. a subconscious oversight

200. Your client, from a family of six children, is extremely conservative and responsible but suffers from feelings of inferiority. According to Alfred Adler's birth-order theory, which place in the family is your client likely to reside?
    a. last born
    b. first born
    c. third born
    d. fifth born

Answers and Explanations

1. A: "inform the patient of the limits of confidentiality." Confidentiality has limits. As a professional counselor, you are ethically bound to report certain things. The patient's intent to hurt someone else, suicidal ideation, and the abuse or neglect of a child are all examples of times when the professional counselor may break confidentiality and report what the patient has disclosed. The first session with a patient should also include a discussion of privacy and specific review of the types of information that would need to be reported, and to whom, given particular situations.

2. C: "jointly decide, between patient and counselor, how the counseling process will proceed." Both counselor and patient should work together in devising the basic counseling plan. Working together, with and open and honest orientation, promotes a more integrated and positive approach to the therapeutic relationship, and furthers the ultimate chances of a successful counseling outcome. A regular review of the counseling plan, and level of progress, is also necessary to ensure a positive therapy outcome and patient satisfaction. This approach also shows respect for the freedom of choice of the patient, and his/her active role in the direction of the counseling relationship.

3. B: "Your personal belief system should not have any bearing on the therapeutic relationship." The personal belief system of the counselor, when engaging in a therapeutic relationship with a client, should not be an issue in therapy. The counselor should be fully aware of his/her belief system and how he/she may diverge from the beliefs of the client in order to keep them in proper perspective. The counselor must avoid allowing those beliefs to impact the counseling process. The focus should be upon the client, and his/her values and belief systems, with a constant respect for individual diversity.

4. D: "accept or decline depending upon the circumstances." Giving a gift is sometimes, and in some cultures, a means of showing respect and gratitude in a way that monetarily compensating the counselor does not. In certain circumstances, accepting a gift may be an acceptable thing for a counselor to do. However, in deciding whether or not to accept a gift, a counselor must consider the client's motivation, the counselor's motivation (in wanting to accept or decline), the monetary value of the item, and of course the point at which the therapeutic relationship has reached. For instance, in some cases declining a gift may be detrimental to therapy. However, for the most part, it is generally best if the counselor does not encourage or accept gifts from those with whom they are in a therapeutic relationship.

5. D: "both A and C." When court-ordered to reveal confidential information about a client, you must of course ethically consider, first and foremost, the counseling relationship, and the rights of the client. You should, if at all possible, obtain written permission from the client to divulge personal information. Failing that, you must use your best professional judgment to limit the amount of information you share with the court. An emphasis must

be placed upon sharing information in a way that would be as respectful as possible toward the confidentiality of your client, and cause the least possible damage to the counseling relationship.

6. C: "accept or decline depending upon the circumstances." A client's file should always be viewed as confidential, and kept in a secure manner and location. There are few exceptions to this requirement that the client's file be kept private, but one would be the request of the client to see his/her own file. In some cases, however, it may be deemed counter to a positive counseling relationship for the client to see the file. In such cases, it is permissible to omit the parts of the file that would prove detrimental. Also, in cases where the client is considered to be incompetent, it would often be best to limit or deny access.

7. D: "be alert to your mental status, and be able to determine if continuing with your clients poses any threat of being detrimental to the counseling process." As a professional and ethical counselor, you should be alert to any and all changes in your mental status. You should be able to detect when changes in your physical, psychological, and/or emotional state may be negatively affecting your ability to competently provide counseling to your clients. You should also be ready and willing to take the necessary measures to remove yourself from counseling should there be the need. You should also be alert to changes in colleagues and willing to assist them with their own impairments, which may affect their counseling ability.

8. A: "it is not considered ethical to perform a forensic evaluation on a current or past client, so you should decline." It is not considered ethical for you to perform forensic evaluations on a past or current client. It is also not considered ethical for you to enter into a counseling situation with someone you have previously performed a forensic evaluation on.

9. D: "yes, you should be able to attend her wedding without a breach of ethics." There is a significant power differential between supervisors and supervisees. As a supervisor, you must be diligently aware of any and all possible circumstances that might negatively affect your ability to competently conduct your role as a supervisor. Some activities can be beneficial to the professional relationship. Activities such as visits to the hospital or attendance at weddings and other significant events may enhance the relationship. However, other activities such as romantic involvements or business investments could prove detrimental and could be considered unethical.

10. B: "yes, you are ultimately responsible." The principal researcher is ultimately responsible for any and all ethical breaches in the research study. All others involved in the research study are individually responsible for their unethical behavior. It is important to note that, individually, everyone involved in a research study must admit personal responsibility, but overall, the principal researcher is responsible for the entirety of the study and anything connected to it.

11. D: "all of the above." When reporting research it is important to always give credit to any other source or individual who has contributed to your work, or from whom you have drawn significant information. Work must also be original (unless indicated otherwise), and one should never plagiarize. Editorial must also be made aware of previous publication of the material, and only one journal should be submitted to at a time. If your material is substantially based on the work of students, they should certainly be listed as principal authors.

12. B: "ultimately, the law may be adhered to over the Code of Ethics." Counselors should make every effort to be knowledgeable of, and adhere to the Code of Ethics as set forth by the ACA. The practice of counselors should remain fully within the bounds of that code, but there may be times when ethics come in conflict with law, regulations, or other forms of authority. When this happens, the counselor is responsible for taking steps to alleviate this conflict. If the counselor's conflict between the ACA Code of Ethics and the rule of law cannot be resolved, then the counselor may adhere to legal authority.

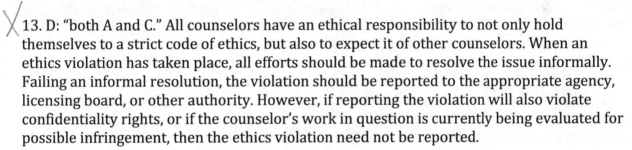

13. D: "both A and C." All counselors have an ethical responsibility to not only hold themselves to a strict code of ethics, but also to expect it of other counselors. When an ethics violation has taken place, all efforts should be made to resolve the issue informally. Failing an informal resolution, the violation should be reported to the appropriate agency, licensing board, or other authority. However, if reporting the violation will also violate confidentiality rights, or if the counselor's work in question is currently being evaluated for possible infringement, then the ethics violation need not be reported.

14. D: "both A and C." It is expected that all counselors respect diversity in their clients, and educate themselves as to the individualistic needs of the clients as affected by such concepts as social identity, history, and economic and political issues, as relevant to particular cultures. Respect for individual cultures and knowledge of their unique and special features are necessary for a counselor to responsibly and ethically provide competent service to their clients.

15. C: "confidentiality." Confidentiality is a major ethical consideration for the mental health professional, and it is also tested the most often. Confidentiality not only affects what is said during counseling sessions, but also involves the storage of records, testimony in court, communication between professionals, and many other areas of practice. The scope of "confidentiality" is so far reaching that it even protects the client after death. When in doubt about any issue related to confidentiality, a counselor should consult the ACA Code of Ethics and other practitioners for assistance. The rules are clear, but situations can sometimes arise that make them difficult to interpret.

16. B: "Erik Erikson." Erik Erikson is responsible for an eight-stage developmental theory. His final stage, "integrity vs despair," starts at age sixty, and each stage includes a turning point (or crisis) of some sort. It is sometimes argued that other theorists, such as Sigmund Freud, also have developmental theories encompassing the full lifespan. However, Freud's final stage still speaks of childhood, and Erik Erikson's theory has a stated stage that clearly

includes the mature adult and the possibility of peak adjustment at that stage, assuming the other stages have been successfully resolved.

17. C: "Sigmund Freud." Sigmund Freud's theory of how the human personality is formed consists of five parts, one of which includes the Id, Ego, and Superego. The Id is all about the "pleasure principle" and animalistic instincts. It's the part of the personality that wants what it wants regardless of the circumstances. The Ego is referred to as the "reality principle" and needs to balance the needs of the Id with the reality of the situation. The Superego is the moral part of the personality, and is concerned with issues of right and wrong.

18. D: "Formal Operations." Jean Piaget's last stage of development, Formal Operations, is when the individual's thinking becomes less tied to reality, and they are more able to use abstract reasoning and formal logic. When faced with a problem during this stage, the child is able to systematically solve problems in a more methodical manner. Jean Piaget theorized that cognitive development is tied to one's ability to process new information. Piaget's stages, in order, are Sensory Motor (involving motor skill and sensory input), Preoperational (increased verbalizations and crudely formed concepts), Concrete Operations (organized thought and logic), and Formal Operations.

19. C: "Erik Erikson." Erik Erikson theorized that adolescents experiment with a variety of roles in an attempt to "find themselves," or determine who they really are. In Erickson's stages of psychosocial development, it is during the teenage years that the individual seeks a clear sense of identity in occupation, politics, religion, and sex roles. The age range for this is considered to be from age twelve to eighteen. The term "identity crisis" has come to be loosely used in society, referring to something that can occur later in the lifespan, but the term originated with Erikson as a feeling during teenage development.

20. A: "the study of the processes that contribute to optimal functioning." Psychology seems to often be about what is abnormal or what has gone wrong in an individual's life. Positive Psychology, however, is about what goes right over the lifespan. It moves the focus from studying abnormal development and problems in everyday living to concentrating on the strengths of individuals and how they can get the most out of life. It is a relatively new area of psychology and still developing. It concentrates on three main areas: positive emotions, positive traits, and positive institutions. The focus is to enhance an individual's experiences in life.

21. C: "orally fixated." Sigmund Freud's psychosexual stages of development consist of five stages. The second stage, the "anal stage," is when the focus is on the anus and the child's sexual gratification is derived from bowel movements. In the "Phallic Stage," the child is fascinated with the penis (or for girls, the lack of). The "Latency Stage" brings with it a period of calm and little conflict, and the "Genital Stage" brings a postpuberty focus on the genitals, maturity, creation of life, and creativity. However, it is the first stage, the "Oral Stage," in which the smoker from our question is likely to be fixated. It is in the Oral Stage that the mouth/sucking is the primary location of pleasure for the individual.

22. B: "that no one theory of development completely explains the process." Each theorist lends a particular emphasis to their theory of development. For instance, Sigmund Freud has a psychosexual bent to it, while Erik Erikson was psychosocial. Lawrence Kohlberg was interested in moral development, and Jean Piaget focused on cognitive issues. Of the various development theorists, each placed their own unique slant on the material, based upon their own experiences and research. Most mental health professionals today see value in all of the theories, discarding some parts and adopting other components in their own practice. Few practitioners, however, would adhere completely to only one developmental theory.

23. D: "attachment theory." John Bowlby was of a psychoanalytic mindset, believing that early experiences had an impact on development and further shaped who one was to become in later life. He theorized that attachment behavior is instinctive, and further formed through the relationship one has as an infant with the primary caregiver. Bowlby also saw an evolutionary element in attachment in that it aids in the individual's ability to survive. He saw problems in infant/childhood attachment as a precursor to other problems in later life. He suggested such issues as delinquency, depression, aggression, affectionless psychopathy, and lowered levels of intelligence as possible problems one might suffer later in life as a result of maternal deprivation.

24. C: "Preconventional, Conventional, and Postconventional." Lawrence Kohlberg was interested in moral development, and theorized stages by which this development occurs in the individual. There are several stages that fall under three "levels." Children begin the Preconventional level by doing whatever they can get away with, and end by beginning to see the needs of others (although still judging everything in terms of their own needs). In the Conventional level, the child acknowledges both others and the rules of society, feeling a duty to obey the rules. In the final level, Postconventional, the individual understands society's role in making decisions, and answers to an inner conscience.

25. B: "the Electra complex." In Sigmund Freud's theory of psychosexual development, the Oedipus complex and Electra complex take place in the Phallic Stage. It is during this stage of development that the child faces his/her greatest sexual conflict. These two complexes refer to the child's unconscious desire to possess the opposite-gender parent, and eliminate the same-sex one. The natural love of child for parent moves toward a sexual energy in the Phallic Stage, thus changing the dynamics of the relationship. This desire remains unconscious; it is repressed.

26. A: "Harry Harlow." Harry Harlow gave us a great understanding of human behavior through his experiments with rhesus monkeys. His famous experiments using a wire/cloth "mother" monkey were done to demonstrate the need for affection being greater than other needs, including the physical. Harlow's work was important not just for the obvious benefits of the research itself, but also for its long-reaching implications, which are used today for abused and neglected children, children who suffer from early losses in their

lives, and other related issues. His work helped to shape how social service agencies, child care workers, adoption agencies, and orphanages care for and manage children today.

27. B: "a theory of human motivation." Maslow was a humanistic psychologist who developed a theory that included five basic, instinctual needs of all human beings. The strongest of the needs is "physiological," because the individual must have these met for basic survival. Once physiological needs are met, the individual can look to "safety" needs to ensure their well-being. Next on the list are needs for "love, affection, and belongingness." Once the most basic of needs are met, individuals can seek to end their loneliness by looking for love and a way to belong. The next need is "esteem" (from self and others), followed by "self-actualization" (to do what one was born to do in life).

28. D: "a chromosomal abnormality." Down syndrome is a common genetic condition causing mental and physical impairment. The most common form is called trisomy 21, which involves an extra copy of the 21st chromosome. There have been many medical and social advances in regards to Down syndrome over the past several years. Many Down syndrome children are now living longer and integrated into the school systems and communities. The physical features and impairments of each case vary significantly, as does intellectual ability. Some require a great deal of supervision and special service, while others may lead relatively healthy and involved lives.

29. A: "Little Albert experiment." John Watson is a well-known behaviorist who believed that any behavior can be learned. He claimed that given any child, and allowed to raise that child however he saw fit, he could make the child turn out however he dictated, regardless of the child's talents and abilities. His most famous experiment involved conditioning a young boy to fear a white rat. He was also able to generalize that fear to other furry, white objects. Watson never deconditioned the child, so the experiment is often used as an example of unethical research. Behavioral modification and conditioning are still widely used today in therapy.

30. C: "Bobo doll study." Albert Bandura stressed imitation, modeling, and observation as the key components in learning. His most famous experiment took place in 1961. It involved showing a group of children a film of a woman beating and shouting angrily at a Bobo doll. The children were then allowed to play in a room that included a Bobo doll, and they would interact with the doll in an aggressive manner, as was modeled for them in the film. Bandura felt this indicated that we learn not just by reinforcement (as behavioral theory suggested), but also by simple observation.

31. B: "cultural context and language." Lev Vygotsky was a Russian psychologist with an interest in development, education, and sociocultural issues. He looked at development in terms of the entire lifespan rather than in stages. Vygotsky believed that the cultural context within which development occurs is critical, and that language plays a large role in that development. In Vygotsky's theory, the social environment an individual resides in has a significant impact upon cognition, with culture playing a major role in the thought patterns of the individual. Vygotsky's ideas are often compared with Jean Piaget's work.

However, Piaget believed that children act independently, while Vygotsky saw social learning as a guiding force.

32. B: "Repression." Sigmund Freud outlined several defense mechanisms. These defense mechanisms are ways that the Ego can defend against levels of anxiety that have become too intense to manage. There are several defense mechanisms, but one of the more commonly referred to is repression. Anna Freud referred to repression as "motivated forgetting," which is a rather clear description of the mechanism. Quite simply, if something is too stressful to deal with, the Ego represses it (forgets it), in order to manage the anxiety. It's important to note that repressed memories do not disappear, but are simply in a type of storage, awaiting retrieval.

33. C: "Konrad Lorenz." Konrad Lorenz is one of Austria's most famous scientists, but he is known in the field of psychology for his work on imprinting. He observed that newly hatched goslings and ducklings would imprint upon whatever they first saw after hatching. The baby birds would later follow and even try to mate with whatever they had imprinted on. Lorenz even tried inanimate objects, which the babies also imprinted on. He felt therefore that the baby birds didn't recognize their species or require reinforcement, so he saw this as innate behavior.

34. B: "eclectic." Most counselors would be considered eclectic because few choose only one theory or method through which they practice their profession. Most mental health professionals will agree that there is value and worth in all of the various theories and research that has taken place in the field of psychology, but also would concede that there are shortcomings to each as well. For that reason, most counselors will rely on several theories for their practice, and will adjust their choices based upon their experience and the population they are serving. Some counselors will base their work with one population on a particular theory, and then use another theory as the base for their work with another.

35. B: "Bipolar." Bipolar disorder most often manifests itself with alternating periods of depressed and elevated mood. While both need not be present for a diagnosis of bipolar disorder, depression and mania are common to many cases. The cycles in bipolar can be of varying lengths, with differing levels of severity. The patient will have symptom-free periods where daily function is at an expected level. The cause of the symptoms must not be medication-related for the diagnosis to be bipolar disorder, and it is often treated with a combination of medication and therapy.

36. A: "Neurocognitive Disorder". The client is exhibiting symptoms of a neurocognitive disorder. He is having cognitive changes without depressive symptoms. His cognitive symptoms have mildly diminished his activities of daily living, but he is able to complete them with modifications, indicating a mild neurocognitive disorder.

37. D: "Schizophrenia, bipolar disorder." Bipolar disorder is primarily a mood disorder, while schizophrenia is characterized more by disordered thought patterns.

38. C: "Rogerian, Client-Centered Therapy." Carl Roger's client-centered approach to therapy mirrors back what the patient is saying, guiding him/her to clearer self-understanding. Rogers believed in freeing clients from obstacles to growth, and aiding them in becoming independent, self-directed individuals. This type of therapy involves a therapist who is more facilitator than director, and only guides clients in making their own decisions. The Rogerian approach involves a positive outlook and high degrees of respect for the client. This type of therapy works well with many types of cases, but is often not the best choice for more severe disorders, such as schizophrenia or other organic disorders.

39. D: "Bulimia." Bulimia is an eating disorder, characterized by periods of binge eating followed by inappropriate methods of avoiding weight gain. The bulimic patient will often lose control of efforts to avoid eating, only to binge uncontrollably. Following the bingeing behavior, the patient will induce diarrhea, vomit, exercise excessively, or any other number of extreme methods. There are many possible causes of bulimia, including body image issues, biological factors, and control issues. Major life changes and stress can also be a factor in bulimic behavior. Cognitive-behavioral therapy is often chosen as a method of treatment, but psychotherapy is also often used.

40. B: "Agoraphobia." While anxiety is certainly present, agoraphobia is more likely the culprit, given the client's feelings of unease while outside the home, and his relative ease while in the home setting. The agoraphobic individual experiences negative physical, psychological, and emotional symptoms when outside his comfort zone (which is often the home setting). In some cases, the symptoms are so severe that the client remains homebound for years, which can lead to secondary difficulties such as relationship and financial problems. The causes of agoraphobia are likely a combination of factors, which are varied. Several treatments are effective, but behavioral techniques, or a combined treatment modality, are likely to be most often utilized.

41. D: "PTSD." Posttraumatic stress disorder (PTSD) is an anxiety disorder that involves the client experiencing anxiety-related symptoms long after the original stressful event took place. Those in the military, crime victims, and survivors of natural disasters are common populations affected by this disorder, as are children who suffer trauma. Flashbacks, nightmares, physical symptoms (eg, intestinal issues, weight gain), and memory and sleep difficulties are just a few of the possible symptoms associated with PTSD. Following evaluation and diagnosis, treatment for PTSD is often psychotherapy and medication. Behavioral techniques, such as desensitization, are also sometimes used effectively.

42. A: Oppositional defiant disorder. The degree of discord is substantial, and the level of verbal conflict is high, thus oppositional defiant disorder would be the most appropriate diagnosis. A parent-child relational problem tends to be less severe in nature, while conduct disorder is much more severe (i.e., involves violations of the rights of others, physical aggression, or property damage, persistent truancy, etc.). Intermittent explosive disorder addresses impulsive acts of aggression or violence (as opposed to premeditated or planned behaviors). Persistent conduct disorder carried into adulthood may meet criteria for antisocial personality disorder.

43. B: "Avoidant personality disorder". The client is describing the features of avoidant personality disorder. Criteria include being worried about social situations, unwillingness to try new activities, avoiding activities once found enjoyable if they are social.

44. C: "Delusional Disorder." Delusional disorder involves non-bizarre delusions in the absence of other mood or psychotic symptoms. These delusions are things that really could happen but simply aren't true. In the psychotic individual, delusions are bizarre (could not happen), so it's important to differentiate between the psychotic delusion and one that takes place without that distinction. It's also important to note that what may seem like a person's "unrealistic belief system" may be acceptable given the culture or religious beliefs of the client. The delusion must be evaluated by taking all factors into account. Psychotherapy and medication are often the choices of treatment for those with a delusional disorder.

45. B: "the cause is unknown." Cyclothymia is a mild form of bipolar disorder. In this disorder, the mood swings from hypomanic behavior to depression symptoms. A client may be resistant to treatment because the hypomanic periods can also result in a significant increase in productivity and positive mood. However, friends and family will likely feel differently. Long-term treatment is necessary with this disorder because, like bipolar disorder, this has a recurring set of symptoms. Medication is often the primary treatment for cyclothymic disorder, but psychotherapy is also useful for support, education, and long-term management of the illness.

46. C: Stimulant use disorder. The DSM-5 no longer separates substances abuse and dependence but now places all disorders under substance use disorder, substance intoxication, and substance withdrawal. Stimulant use disorder involves the need for escalating amounts of a substance to achieve intoxication, withdrawal symptoms, compulsive use in spite of a desire to stop, compromised social, occupational/educational, familial, and/or other important role compromise due to the use of an intoxicating substance, and includes severe physiological or compulsive use features. Severity is decided by the number of symptoms, and can be classified as mild, moderate, or severe.

47. B: Malingering. Malingering involves feigning symptoms primarily to derive an <u>external reward</u> (lawsuit settlement, disability benefits, etc.). Illness anxiety disorder involves a misapprehension or misinterpretation of bodily symptoms. Factitious disorder involves a feigning of symptoms primarily in order to receive the attention offered when one assumes a sick role, even in the absence of external reward. Somatic symptom disorder is characterized by complaints regarding several organ systems involving different body sites and functions rather than a single body organ or situation.

48. D: "positive, negative, and disorganized." The symptoms of schizophrenia create a significant change in the patient's personality, and are characterized in three ways. "Positive" symptoms are things that should not be present (such as delusions and hallucinations). Symptoms characterized as "negative" are missing aspects that should be

present (such as "normal" emotional reactions or speech patterns). "Disorganized" symptoms would be issues such as inability to communicate with others appropriately or difficulty interpreting others.

49. C: Borderline personality disorder. The key features of BPD involved instability in relationships and affect, poor self-image, and high impulsivity. Violations of personal rights and apathy common to antisocial personality disorder are insufficiently pronounced. While evidence of histrionic behavior exists, the devaluation/over-valuation pattern common to BPD is not accounted for via histrionic personality disorder. Nor is the need for admiration, pervasive with narcissism, not otherwise addressed.

50. A: "increased." Suicide ideation is often a result of depression. When depressed, the patient will show significant changes to his usual behavior, which could include changes in eating, sleeping habits, work behavior, relationship problems, and many other possible factors. When a patient has been in the midst of a depression for some time, and suicide has been a significant factor, one of the times the risk is highest is when the patient appears to suddenly feel better. Friends and relatives will often drop their guard at that time, but it is then that the patient is more likely to attempt suicide because he/she made the final decision, feels the relief of being out of conflict, and is ready to act.

51. A: Schizophrenia. Typical symptoms include: grossly disorganized or catatonic behavior and/or speech, delusions and/or hallucinations, blunted affect (poor or inappropriate expressive responses to external stimuli), autism (intense self-preoccupation). Continuous signs of symptoms must be present (allowing for waxing and waning fluctuations) for six or more months. There are five types: 1) paranoid; 2) disorganized; 3) catatonic; 4) undifferentiated; and, 5) residual. Early mild symptoms are sometimes referred to as prodromal schizophrenia. Common medications for treatment: Clozaril (clozapine), Haldol (haloperidol), Loxitane (loxapine), Mellaril (thioridazine), Prolixin (fluphenazine), Risperdal (risperidone), Stelazine (trifluoperazine), Thorazine (chlorpromazine), and Zyprexa (olanzapine).

52. A. "Conversion disorder" (which is sometimes still referred to as hysterical neurosis) occurs when psychological stress is converted into a physical symptom. There must be no physical cause of the physical symptom for the diagnosis of conversion disorder to be made. Most of the time, physical symptoms will occur quite suddenly following a stressful event or experience. They can be as simple as a lump in the throat or as debilitating as a paralysis of a limb. The exact cause of conversion disorder is unknown, and treatment is often psychotherapy and stress management.

53. D: "any of the above." Appraisal can be any means by which a counselor assesses the client. Sometimes the assessment may be in the form of an IQ test, mental status exam, psychodynamic evaluation, group test, or even just clinical interview and observation. Testing can be used to aid the client in choosing a career, point toward possible psychological disorders, or place a child in an appropriate class (given intelligence level or

disabilities). Appraisal is simply a way to collect information about the client so that the counselor can be more effective in the therapeutic relationship.

54. A: "objective." The National Counselor Examination is a four-hour, paper and pencil test, using a multiple-choice format. The test is given twice a year in various locations, and used by many states as a way to determine eligibility to be certified as a professional counselor. It's an objective test because the personal thoughts and feelings of the test-takers are not taken into account. The individual taking the test simply chooses from among the four choices offered for each question. The word "objective" refers to the scoring method used with the particular test, and there is only one right answer to each question.

55. A: "IQ." The Wechsler IQ test is a general test of cognitive ability. David Wechsler developed his first intelligence test, the Wechsler-Bellevue test, in 1939. That was replaced in 1955 by the Wechsler Adult Intelligence Scale (WAIS). In 1981 it was revised and called the WAIS-R. Another update took place in 1997, called the WAIS-III. The test has eleven different subtests, and versions specific to country. The test result includes a "verbal IQ" score, a "performance IQ" score, and a "full scale IQ" score to give a well-rounded view of the individual's intellectual level and abilities.

56. B: "inform the client of the limitations of testing." Testing results can be affected by many factors. They also provide information collected at a particular point in time and in a particular situation, where many factors can affect the results. For ethical reasons, the patient should be informed of the limitations of testing, and made as comfortable as possible with the testing situation and results. The counselor should also keep in mind the limitations of the testing results, and not rely too heavily on any one test or test results.

57. D: "how accurate a test is." The "validity" of a test tells how useful it will be, or in other words, if the test is really measuring what one wants it to measure. When speaking of validity in testing, several types of validity are often referred to. "Construct validity" is how well the test measures the "construct" that it was designed to measure. In "concurrent validity," "convergent validity" tells one whether or not the test will give results similar to other tests like it, and "divergent validity" will reveal if the test gives different results from tests that measure different constructs. Any particular construct consists of a number of factors that must be taken into account, and a test's "content validity" tells one if the test takes those factors into consideration. Finally, "criterion-related validity" refers to the test's ability to predict the client's performance.

58. C: "how consistent the test results are." Reliability tells one if the test is able to give consistent results each time it is administered. A problem with determining this comes into play with the "memory factor" (as the same group may remember some of the answers during subsequent administrations), which can affect the validity of the test. There are also other types of reliability. For instance, "test-retest reliability" refers to the administration of the test, and "internal-consistency reliability" is about how the items of the test relate to each other.

59. C: "disregard the results of the test as the reliability is too low." Reliability levels of .60 or below are often considered to be too low to be acceptable. Lower levels can be acceptable only if you are using the information gained from the test in conjunction with other tests or information, and should not be considered if you are using it as the primary source of information about the client. A high reliability is considered .90, with .80 as moderate and .79 as low reliability. A reliability of .60 would be considered by most to be too low to be of significant use.

60. B: "inherited intellectual abilities." Francis Galton was a British psychologist. Charles Darwin was his cousin, and perhaps encouraged by his cousin's writings, Galton developed a keen interest in heredity. Just as in Darwin's work with the plant and animal world, Galton hypothesized that individual personality traits (and particularly intellectual superiority), were inherited. In 1869, Galton's book *Hereditary Genius* outlined his belief that superior abilities and intellect were handed down generation to generation. He is often called "the father of behavioral genetics" for his work with twins, and also founded the first mental testing center.

61. C: "individual differences and intellect." J. P. Guilford was an American psychologist known primarily for his study of intellectual ability and individual differences. He also did research in creativity, which he associated with "divergent thinking." He believed that intelligence testing wouldn't be as effective with divergent thinking/creative people so he developed special tests for divergent thinkers, which are used with gifted children and others. He believed that creative people could actually achieve lower IQ scores because of the manner in which they approached the testing. He was one of the early theorists who believed intelligence to be a complex, diverse issue, and that a variety of differences and abilities must be taken into account.

62. A: "Alfred Binet and Theophilus Simon." The first intelligence test was developed in 1905 by Alfred Binet and Theophilus Simon. They began work on the test as a means to identify students with low intellectual abilities who could benefit from specialized education. Work continued on the test for some time following. The Stanford-Binet Intelligence Scale was developed out of that original test, and consists of four areas: verbal reasoning, quantitative reasoning, abstract/visual reasoning, and short-term memory. A larger, more diverse sample was used in its development, and it improved upon the original test by further correcting for racial and gender issues.

63. C: "the inkblot test." The Rorschach test was introduced in 1921 by Herman Rorschach. It came to be known as the "inkblot test" because the test consists of ten cards, each with the picture of an inkblot on them. Most are shades of black and grey, but a few have some color on them. The client tells the clinician what he sees in each inkblot, and the test is used to determine information about the client's personality. It is a very popular test in psychology, but is considered by some to be unreliable. Other tests similar to it have also been developed in recent years.

64. B: "MMPI." The Minnesota Multiphasic Personality Inventory (MMPI) is one of the most researched psychological tests. It was developed in the 1930s by Starke R. Hathaway and J.C. McKinley at the University of Minnesota. The MMPI is used for a variety of reasons, including in the criminal justice system, for determining suitability in some professions, and in child custody cases. However, it is most often used in determining psychological disorders. The test consists of ten scales, each focusing on a particular psychological disorder. There are also validity scales to highlight when a client is lying, or trying to influence the score one way or another, and other safeguards to aid in the interpretation of the results.

65. C: "psychological measurement." Psychology studies the inner workings of the mind and behavior, but psychometrics seeks to measure it. Psychometrics involves the design, administration, and interpretation of psychological testing. The testing could measure intelligence, traits, disorders, or any other number of psychology-related factors. Sir Francis Galton is often credited as the first pioneer in the field of psychometrics, with a free-association experiment he conducted and later wrote about in 1879. Charles Spearman developed that early work into the idea of measuring human intelligence. Alfred Binet later created an intelligence test, and from there the idea was developed and refined further. Today, psychometrics is a popular field of study, and a valuable tool for clinicians.

66. B: "a personality test." The Myers-Briggs Type Indicator (MBTI) is a test based upon the theory of Carl Jung, and measures personality types. It looks at sixteen distinct personality types. The test is considered to be both valid and reliable, and is very simple to administer. The MBTI does not make judgments about the different types of personalities, but rather is a means by which to understand the differences and similarities among types of people. Analysis of the test can be useful to the client in terms of issues such as self-awareness, career choice, and personal relationships.

67. C: "Carl Jung." Carl Jung, a student of Sigmund Freud, developed the Word Association Test (WAT). In the WAT, a single word is read to the client, who then responds as quickly as possible with whatever word comes to mind. The word the client responds with is recorded, but other factors are also noted such as speed of response and client behavior. The test was used to clarify issues of psychopathology, but also as a means of generally gleaning information about the client's personality. The WAT has also been used in the study of memory. The test was based on earlier ideas of mental associations.

68. C: "an aptitude test." The terms "aptitude test" and "achievement test" are often used interchangeably, but they are quite different from each other. Achievement is what one can do, while aptitude is what one has the ability to do. In the achievement test, the test measures what the subject currently knows. It is the type of test commonly used in the school setting. In the norm-referenced achievement test, the subject is measured against others who also took the test. In a criterion-referenced achievement test, the subject is measured against a previously set criterion. Aptitude tests differ from achievement tests in that they measure the subject's ability or interests in particular areas. Career testing would

be a common example of an aptitude test that helps subjects choose a career based upon their interests.

69. B: "after the 1960s." Prior to the 1960s, psychological problems were seen as best dealt with through individual therapy. The concept of group therapy naturally evolved out of other group dynamics that have been present throughout history. Religious groups, fraternal organizations, schools, and even the basic family unit have all reflected both the positive and negative attributes of group dynamics. It was to be expected that psychology would also embrace the group setting as a means by which to deal with personal and interpersonal issues, and a great deal of progress has been made in the professional treatment of individuals within the group therapy setting.

70. A: "Alfred Adler." Alfred Adler is considered by many as one of the founding fathers of psychology. Both Sigmund Freud and Carl Jung (the other two founding fathers) talked about intrapsychic dynamics, focusing on the internal processes of the individual and using individual therapy as a treatment modality. However, Alfred Adler did not. Adler looked at the individual in relation to his/her environment, and so it was natural for him to embrace a less individualized approach to therapy. As early as the 1920s, he was already involved in use of group therapy.

71. C: "homogeneous, closed group." A homogeneous group is one in which the members share a similarity. By contrast, the heterogeneous group is one made up of individuals who may not share a commonality. An open group allows new members to join throughout the therapy sessions, but a closed group does not admit new members to the group once the group therapy sessions have begun. The length of the group therapy sessions, the number of sessions, and any other factors are not dictated by these distinctions. Some types of groups, with particular populations, are more effective with one type of group or another, and the decision of which to offer should be made on a case-by-case basis.

72. D: "Both A and B." The closed group promotes greater cohesiveness within the group because of the stability of the membership. With the same members interacting with each other during each session, the group members can form closer relationships, and will have fewer inhibitions as time goes by. There is a lack of diversity/change, but that can be a good thing depending upon the dynamics and goals of the group setting. The closed group is less cost-effective because as members may drop out or miss sessions, you will not be able to replace them with new paying members.

73. A: "not setting firm goals for the group." Co-leaders of different gender can actually be a strength in the group setting. Likewise, noting possible problems in potential members is not always an issue, as they can used within the group dynamics to the enhancement of the group process. A problem arises however, when firm goals are not set for the group. Depending upon the leader and members, it can be easy for the goals to be diluted if firm goals aren't set and adhered to at the start of the sessions. It takes a strong facilitator to keep the focus on the goals and move the group ahead.

74. B: "to expand practical understanding of group work." R.K. Conyne felt that the understanding of the range of group experiences found in group therapy was lacking, and the Group Work Grid is a result of that concern. The Group Work Grid is composed of two dimensions. One level address the level of the group intervention work, and the other refers to the purpose of the group work. "Purpose" is further divided into correction and enhancement subcategories, while the level of the group work is further composed of individual, organizational, interpersonal, and community. The Group Work Grid provides a working model of group typology that has depth and practical application for the clinician.

75. B: "online psychological treatment." E-therapy is also sometimes called cyber-therapy, e-counseling, tele-therapy, or just online therapy or counseling. It can involve either individual or group therapy, and is accomplished in a number of ways. Videoconferencing, chat rooms, e-mail, and instant messaging are some of the more common methods of providing counseling services. As e-therapy is still a new manner of conducting therapy, it is often met with skepticism by some professionals and clients. However, e-therapy is a dramatically growing field and makes therapy possible for many patients who are otherwise unwilling, or unable to, attend the traditional therapy session.

76. A: "have an outside observer assess the group." An effective method to evaluate the progress of a group therapy session is to have an outside observer sit in on a session or two, and evaluate the group dynamics. Using the group facilitator or counselor to evaluate the group may not always be the most effective method, as the counselor would be evaluating his/her own performance. Likewise, group members are ineffective at evaluating the group because of their personal involvement and possible lack of objectivity. An outside observer brings an objective view to the situation, and can more easily point out possible difficulties between group members, and between the group and the facilitator.

77. A: "parents." When involved in therapy with children, it is often useful to include parents in the sessions. There are several reasons why this can be a positive addition to therapy. Parents provide an added sense of security for the child, especially in cases in which the child is very young. In cases in which the child is shy or fearful, the initial inclusion of a parental figure can be critical to the success of future sessions, as it eases the child into a relationship with the counselor (that can later more effectively become independent of parental involvement). In cases in which a child is resistant to therapy or even aggressive, the presence of a parent can aid the counselor in obtaining a reasonable level of cooperation from the child.

78. C: "a role assumed by a group therapy member." A variety of roles are seen in group therapy dynamics. These roles often assist in the proper performance of the group. The "gatekeeper" is a type of "maintenance" role within the group. Maintenance roles address the socio-emotional aspects of the entire group. In terms of the gatekeeper specifically, he/she is the group member who organizes and leads. He/she may also encourage other members of the group, making sure they each get a chance to speak their mind, and keep communication open. Other common "maintenance" roles within the group are the Harmonizer, Supporter, and Compromiser, among others.

79. A: "nonassertive." Someone who is nonassertive within the group therapy setting is quite the same as someone who is nonassertive in other situations. The goal of the passive, nonassertive individual is to avoid conflict and be liked by others. For this reason, the nonassertive person is likely to agree with what others say, or at least give the impression that he does. This type of interaction may serve to avoid and/or diffuse conflict. However, others in the group may not always react positively toward the nonassertive individual because they have a hard time knowing what the nonassertive person really feels and believes, and they also may not respect the nonassertive person because of his/her passive behavior.

80. D: "storming." There are several stages common to group therapy dynamics. Forming is the initial stage when group members are first placed together, and members tend to be rather cautious during this stage. The second stage is called Storming, when group members begin to familiarize themselves with each other and test limits. Norming occurs when conflicts begin to be worked out, and some level of cohesiveness is achieved. In the Performing stage, the group is at its most mature and working toward common goals. The final stage is Adjourning, and is just as it sounds, the act of disbanding the group.

81. D: "a group member who blocks new ideas." A "Blocker" is one of several "self-oriented roles" that involve the group member's concern about their own place in the group dynamics rather than the progress of the group as a whole. The Blocker tends to waste the group's time with old issues, and is almost always negative, as well as resistant to new ideas. Other self-oriented roles would be those who are aggressive or seek attention. Some members also avoid issues or remain passive in the group setting, and there are others who may tend to dominate the group discussion, turning discussions back toward themselves and their own issues.

82. D: "both A and B." Clients who are in the midst of a personal crisis, suicidal, psychotic, sociopathic, or in other ways significantly impaired are often not good candidates for group therapy. Clients with traumatic brain injury or who are intellectually impaired also may not be good candidates. A client who is in the midst of a personal crisis, or otherwise fragile, is best treated with individual therapy until at a point where they are stable enough to join the group dynamic. Patients who enter a group situation before they are ready run the risk of dropping out or experiencing an exacerbation of their symptoms. They may also impede the group process for the other members.

83. B: "analysis of the group's interactions." "Group Process" refers to the interaction of the group members and analysis of how that interaction is working in terms of the group's goals. What the group members say to each other verbally, behavioral cues, and other factors are all taken into account in the interpretation of the group therapy sessions. This includes relationship issues, adherence to goals, individual and group progress, and a variety of other factors that made up the group dynamic.

84. C: "the material that is being discussed within the group." "Group Content" refers to the content being discussed among the group members in the group therapy session. This is different from Group Process, which refers to how the material and interactions between members are progressing in terms of the group's goals. Put simply, Group Content is what is said, and Group Process is the analysis of the content.

85. C: "6 and 8." Most groups seem to function best with six to eight members. However, for groups involving children or adolescents, a slightly smaller group may be advantageous. Likewise, with online group therapy, group size is often thought to be best if kept smaller. In cases of groups that are long-running, there will sometimes be a larger number of members participating in the group, but smaller tends to be the better choice. Keeping groups small allows for more interaction between members, increased time for each individual to be heard, and enhanced opportunity for the group leader to manage the group.

86. D: "Social Psychology." Social Psychology deals primarily with groups and other social factors. This area of psychology studies issues such as how individuals behave in group settings, how social interaction affects the individual, and how the individual impacts upon society. Simply put, Social Psychology combines Psychology and Sociology. While Psychology studies the individual and internal processes, Social Psychology looks more at the individual's connections to others in society. This discipline believes that society plays a large role in how the individual views himself, his place in the world, and his behavior, as well as the choices he makes.

87. D: "Emile Durkheim." Emile Durkheim is considered by many to be the father of sociology. He is often credited with making sociology a science, and he conducted a great deal of research and educational endeavors on the subject, as well as wrote books and gave many lectures. He was one of the first sociologists to make use of statistical and scientific techniques. Durkheim believed that all parts of the society work together as a machine, which came to be known as "sociological functionalism." He is also known for his studies of religion, labor, crime, and suicide.

88. A: "yes." A counselor can enter into a therapeutic relationship with a client, even if that client is culturally different. In such a situation, the term "cultural relativity" comes into play. Cultural relativity basically refers to the belief that a situation is relative to the culture in which it occurs. In the counseling setting, the therapist would address the issues presented by the client in terms of the client's culture. It would not be appropriate to do otherwise. For example, something that would be acceptable in the counselor's culture may not be acceptable from the client's perspective. Therefore, applying the client's issues to the counselor's culture would not be relevant (or helpful).

89. B: "the study of proximity." Proxemics is the study of proximity. It refers to personal and interpersonal space and territoriality. Proxemics studies how an individual's proximity to others and things impacts that individual. The term was introduced by the anthropologist Edward Hall in 1966. He found there were measurable distances between

people based upon specific circumstances and interactions. Proxemics defines certain types of space: fixed-feature, semi-fixed feature, and informal space. It also defines intimate, personal, social, and public distances, as well as specifying a variety of behavioral categories.

90. C: "Asian." An Asian client is most likely to choose a counselor who is Asian because individuals are likely to form connections with others who are most like themselves. In Social Psychology, the research into issues such as this tends to indicate that similarity leads to attraction. People tend to feel that their feelings and beliefs are validated by relationships with others who are similar to who they are. Studies have been done regarding such factors as communication, demographics, opinions, and value systems to indicate that those who are similar attract. While not always the case, an Asian client would likely be most comfortable with an Asian as a counselor.

91. C: "attribution." An area of study in social cognition is attribution. Attribution refers to the explanations people make for the behaviors that people engage in. Internal attributions deal with factors within the individual. External attributions assign the cause of behavior to outside factors. Generally people tend to assign external causes for their failures in life, and internal causes to the failures of others. The success of others is often also seen as the result of external elements, while one's own success may more likely be attributed to internal causes.

92. A: "how people are supposed to act." A statistical norm would measure how people actually act, but a cultural norm is all about expectations and how people are supposed to behave in that particular culture. In fact, some professionals suggest that it is simply a group of cultural norms that makes a particular culture. Social norms are expected to be adhered to within a culture, and there is usually a penalty for breaking those norms. A norm may be something like the style of clothing that is appropriate to wear in a given situation (like wearing black to a funeral in the United States), or taking your place at the end of a customer service line instead of just cutting into the front of the line. Breaking accepted, and expected, cultural norms can result in simple irritation on the part of others or even in being ostracized from the culture.

93. B: "people will usually obey authority." Following WWII, a common excuse used to explain some of the terrible acts committed was that the individual was just following orders. Inspired by this supposition, Stanley Milgram (in the 1960s) set out to explore the issue of authority and obedience. In his famous experiment, Milgram found that the majority of people, when faced with someone of authority, will do as they are told—even to the detriment of someone else. His experiment raised ethical issues about the treatment of subjects in psychological experiments, but the study itself is still heralded today as a significant contribution to the field of social psychology.

94. C: "Emory Bogardus." The Social Distance Scale is a technique developed by Emory Bogardus in the 1930s to measure social distance. It's usually thought of as related to issues of prejudice. The scale asks an individual to agree or disagree with a number of

- 52 -

statements about a particular group. It looks at factors such as intimacy, warmth, hostility, and indifference. The scale measures a person's willingness to connect socially with different groups depending upon their social closeness to someone from that group. Bogardus found negative attitudes toward Turks, African-Americans, and Jewish and Mexican groups in his study. A replication of the study in 1947 found that those attitudes were still present.

95. A: "compliance." The "foot-in-the-door" technique is attributed to Freedman and Fraser and their 1966 study. In their study they asked people if they could put a large, unattractive sign about safe driving in their front yard. When simply asked outright, most people said no. However, when people were first asked to sign a safe-driving petition, they were more likely to comply with the sign being placed on their front yard. The smaller request was, in effect, the "foot-in-the-door" for the researchers that later gained them what they really wanted. The idea is that if you begin by making a small request of someone, you are more likely to get him to agree to something big. Without leading up to your large request, you are less likely to secure compliance.

96. A: "the false becomes true." The "self-fulfilling prophecy" is attributed to the sociologist Robert Merton in his book *Social Theory and Social Structure*. The idea is that the act of predicting something (even though not true at the time of the prediction) can make it eventually come true. Behavior as a result of the false prediction begins to change because of it, and be seen as proof of it actually being true, which the prediction eventually becomes. For example, telling a teacher that a particular student is gifted may cause her to behave differently toward him (enhanced attention and reinforcement perhaps), which may eventually lead to the student performing better than he would have. Thus the false prediction becomes true.

97. D: "Social Identity Theory." Social Identity Theory basically says that when individuals belong or are assigned to a group, they tend to think of that group as elite or special. People want to have a positive self-image, so identifying themselves with the elite group makes them feel they are better than others. Social Identity theory is attributed to Henry Tajfel. Tajfel's theory is used to explain conflict and prejudice between groups. He was a European Jew who survived World War II, and his theory developed out of his attempts to explain the violence he had experienced as a part of his "group."

98. B: "social exchange theory." Social Exchange Theory reduces altruism to the simple factors of cost and gain. The theory says that people do things for those people from whom they can expect something in return. Of course, this theory does not explain all instances of altruistic behavior, but it does point to the reason for some altruistic acts. In fact, some professionals theorize that there is no such thing as a purely altruistic act.

99. C: "consensual validity." When the thoughts and behaviors of two people are similar, they validate each other. In other words, each feels good in the presence of the other because of their similarities. Consensual validity is the term for this interpersonal dynamic, which helps to explain why people are attracted to those who are like them. Being similar

also has the advantage of allowing for the enjoyment of common activities, and the increased ability to control the relationship (because of the increased understanding of how the other person thinks and feels), which also lends to the attraction.

100. A: "cognitive dissonance." Leon Festinger, a social psychologist, developed the concept of cognitive dissonance. It refers to an individual's desire to avoid inconsistency and always move toward consistency. For example, when a man behaves in a manner that is inconsistent with his belief system, he will feel anxiety and seek to eliminate, or minimize, that anxiety. He will either seek to change his behavior, or come up with some reasons to justify his behavior. Those reasons, while not changing the original cause of the anxiety, will serve to at least help him to feel better about his behavior.

101. D: "Both A and C." According to the contingency model of leadership, an individual becomes a leader because of both personality issues and situational factors. It further states that both leaders and followers influence each other. In this model, leaders either focus their leadership duties on completing particular tasks or direct their attention toward the relationship between the members of the group. Which style is best, according to this model, is dependent upon the situation. A task-oriented leadership style is better if the situation is harsh, with the relationship style better in easier times.

102. A: "more." One of the most widely studied aspects of altruism is the question of why one person helps a person in need when another will not. The "bystander effect" says that people are more likely to help someone in need if no one else is present. Many studies of bystander intervention show that the majority of people will step in to help someone if there is no one else around to do so. Possible explanations for this effect is that people may look to others for information on how to act, or they may feel the other will act for them.

103. B: "approach/avoidance." There are three main types of conflict that can cause great stress. Approach/approach, avoidance/ avoidance, and approach/avoidance are the three types of conflict. In this case, the conflict is one of approach/avoidance. The client loves sweets, but yet also hates the sweets for what they cause to happen. So, in essence, the client approaches the source of conflict, and also avoids it. Avoidance/avoidance is when both circumstances are negative, yet one must be chosen. With approach/approach, the individual must choose between two positive situations.

104. A: "two cultures mix." Acculturation takes place when two different cultures mix together and begin to change. Cultural exchange goes in both directions, but there is usually more change in the smaller, less dominant culture. Because of the changes to the less-dominant culture, there is usually also more stress on that cultural group, which may lead to other problematic issues. In regards to mental health issues related to acculturation, studies have shown a variety of levels of impact, depending upon the particular circumstances. Acculturation issues have been discussed as far back as Plato, and have been increasingly studied through recent years.

105. D: "A and B." The Likert Scale was developed in 1932 by Renis Likert, and is a psychometric, multi-item scale used for questionnaires. Likert wanted to develop a scientific way in which to measure psychological attitudes, and the factors that influence those attitudes and feelings. The scale is commonly used in surveys and other studies in which closed-ended questions are desired (ones that don't allow the respondent to answer in their own words). A Likert Scale survey asks the respondent to choose where on a scale (ranging from "strongly disagree" to "completely agree") their attitudes lie.

106. C: "inductive reasoning." Reasoning is a means by which one processes information in order to reach a conclusion. There are several forms of reasoning, two of which are inductive reasoning and deductive reasoning. Inductive reasoning is reasoning that flows from the specific to the general, such as knowing something about one member of a group, and then generalizing that to the entire group the individual belongs to. Deductive reasoning is the opposite. In deductive reasoning, knowledge of a particular group is generalized to each of the individuals within that group. It is of course, not best to rely on only one type of reasoning to reach a conclusion.

107. B: "an operational definition." The operational definition allows researchers to understand how something is being measured. Happiness, for example, cannot be simply measured. However, measuring the number of smiles in a day is one possible operational definition of how to measure happiness. An operational definition is very important in psychological research, because without it an experiment or study could not be replicated. It is important for replication to be done if a study is to be considered scientific. The operational definition tells the reader exactly how the study was done so that it can be carefully and methodically replicated in the future.

108. A: "random sampling." Random sampling is a very basic form of probability sampling and is commonly known. It involves samples being drawn from a population in which the entire population has an equal chance of being chosen for the sample. Usually each element from the population is selected only once ("without replacement"), but sometimes the item may be returned to the population and has the chance of being selected once again. Random sampling seems very simple in theory, but can be difficult because all of the elements of the population must be identified first before they can be sampled.

109. A: "a cross-sectional study." A cross-sectional study involves a research study using people who are similar in all areas except the variable that is being studied. For instance, one might wish to measure the intelligence level of a group of people of differing ages. However, measuring the intelligence level of differing ages during the same year does not account for lifestyle issues, differing resources that were available to the older subjects vs the younger ones, etc. This is one of the criticisms of cross-sectional studies. Longitudinal studies are often preferred because they measure a variable over the lifespan (or a number of years) of each particular subject.

110. D: "both B and C." In observational research, the results can be biased by the measurement itself. The "observer effect" is a type of measurement effect. It refers to the

subjects in the research study behaving differently because they know they are being observed. The Hawthorne effect came about as a result of a workplace study near Chicago in the 1950s, and the term was coined by Henry Landsberger. A study had been commissioned to determine if workers would be more productive in more light or less light. The study showed that light levels didn't matter because simply knowing they were being studied caused the employees to work harder.

111. B: "the placebo effect." A placebo is a substance that is generally used in one of two ways. It can be used as a control in an experiment to determine the true effectiveness of a medication. A placebo can also be used as a substitute for a medication, and meant to work based on the expectation of the subject using the placebo. Many studies have shown that giving a placebo is preferable to providing no treatment at all, and that many patients favorably respond to placebos. Some professionals believe that the use of placebos is unprofessional, and its use in psychotherapy is controversial. However, even though not completely understood, it has been shown to be beneficial in some cases.

112. A: "WAIS-IV." The WAIS is the Wechsler Intelligence Scale for those over the age of sixteen, and is the IQ test for adults. It was developed by David Wechsler and began in 1939 as the Wechsler-Bellevue Scale. In 1955 the WAIS replaced that original test, and has gone through several revisions since that time. The eleven subtests of the WAIS address both verbal (six subtests) and performance (five subtests) abilities. The subject receives scaled scores for each of the subtests, and then an overall performance IQ score, verbal IQ score, and a full scale IQ score.

113. D: "WISC-R." The WISC is the Wechsler Intelligence Scale for Children, and tests the intellectual ability of children from age six to sixteen. It was developed by David Wechsler and has gone through revisions since its origination. The test is commonly used today to determine intellectual impairment, or gifted status, for school-aged children. It is also used to determine the presence of neurological impairment. The test consists of several subtests in both "verbal" and "performance" categories, and provides scaled scores on the subtests, as well as an overall verbal IQ, performance IQ, and full-scale IQ score.

114. B: "it shows the number of times a particular value occurs." A frequency distribution presents data in a way that one can see how often a particular value occurs. Likewise, in a grouped frequency distribution, groups of items or categories are shown. There commonly are also cumulative frequency distributions that address a set of data. The frequency distribution is important because it's a way to organize and make sense of a multitude of data. Some common ways to present the data in a frequency distribution is through a bar graph, frequency polygon, and a frequency curve.

115. C: "average." The Wechsler Adult Intelligence Scale (WAIS-IV) consists of several subtests divided between "verbal" and "performance" categories. The results of the test include three scaled scores, which are a verbal IQ score, a performance IQ score, and a full-scale IQ score. A full-scale score of 130 and above indicates a subject performing in the "very superior" range. 120 to 129 is the "superior" range, 110 to 119 is "high average," and

90 to 109 is "average." The "borderline" range is a score of 70 to 79, with 69 and below being in the "extremely low" range.

116. B: "mild to moderate intellectual disabilities." The Diagnostic and Statistical Manual of Mental Disorders classifies intellectual disabilities in relation to Wechsler IQ scores. A score of 50 to approximately 79 indicates mild intellectual disability. Moderate intellectual disability is 35 to 55, with severe intellectual disability falling between the scores of 20 and 40. Profound intellectual disability is below 20 or 25. Of course, you can see by the overlap of the ranges that the number itself is not enough to make a determination. A number of factors besides the subject's score must be taken into consideration in determining the subject's true level of impairment, such as communication skills, self-care, and self-direction, to name just a few.

117. D: "both A and B." An independent variable is the experimental factor in an experiment. It is the element in the experiment that is changed or manipulated. It's called "independent" because it can be changed without affecting other variables. By contrast, the dependant variable in an experiment is the one that is measured, and watched in relation to what is done with the independent variable. If the dependent variable is changed by the manipulation of the independent variable, one might conclude that the independent variable had an effect upon the dependant variable. Of course one must still determine if one actually caused the other.

118. A: "how strong the relation is between things." The more closely related two things are, the greater the number of predictions that can be made about each from the other. A correlation strategy seeks to determine how strong the relation is between things. For example, one might wish to conduct an experiment related to health issues, and therefore propose that high levels of stress and high blood pressure go together. Although that statement alone doesn't mean that one causes the other, it does provide valuable information and further the scientific study of that issue.

119. B: "pairs of scores." A scatter plot (or scattergram) is a type of graph that depicts pairs of scores. The x-axis of the graph shows one variable and the y-axis records the other. Each dot that is "scattered" around on the graph depicts a pair of scores collected in the experiment. The scatterplot makes it easy to see a pattern among the scores, but generally limits one to a broad generalization about the data. The scatter plot is valued in research because you can instantly see a positive or negative relationship between the data, and if that relationship is strong or weak. You can also easily see if the relationship is a linear one.

120. D: "all of the above." A correlation coefficient is a number that shows the degree of relationship between the two variables studied in an experiment. The numeric value of the correlation coefficient falls between +1.00 and -1.00, and there are two parts to each. The number of the correlation coefficient reveals how strong the relationship between two factors is—the closer the number is to 1.00, the stronger the correlation is (regardless of the sign). The closer the number of the correlation coefficient is to .00, the weaker the relationship. The sign (plus or minus) shows the direction of the two variables'

relationship. A negative correlation's variables vary in opposite directions. A positive correlation's variables vary in the same direction.

121. D: "statistically significant." Conducting scientific studies is important for the advancement of knowledge in psychology. However, how does one know if those studies, and the results of those studies, are trustworthy? A statistical significance means that the differences between two variables are great enough that it's not likely that those differences are due to chance. A minimum level of statistical significance of .05 is often necessary for concluding that the differences seen aren't simply a fluke. In fact, when you hear that a test is statistically significant, they're saying that there is a 95% chance that the experiment's results are not due to chance.

122. A: "limitations in the workplace." The "glass ceiling" refers to career limits that restrict a worker's ability to rise above a certain professional level. The term is usually used in relation to women or minorities, who some believe are oppressed by white males. This is complex issue, not easily explained. For example, some hypothesize that differences in income level and professional status between white males and those with ethnic and gender differences may be due to other factors (such as leaving the workforce for periods of time to raise children). Some also suggest that the expectation of the existence of the glass ceiling may actually cause workers to withdraw from the workforce. Cause and effect, in relation to the glass ceiling, is still debated.

123. D: "all of the above." In the past, work was viewed as a way to earn a wage in order to support a family. In recent years, however, choice of "work" has become more an issue of self-expression than simply a means to earn a living. Individuals now view the type of work they do as an extension of who they are. Social expectations often assume that an individual will choose work that they like, and that they are good at, rather than simply one that pays a good wage. Particular careers are also seen to exude a certain status, which also may be valued more the need to support oneself or a family.

124. A: "time away from work." Past generations worked long hours, focusing on wages and the need to support a family. However, in recent years, the focus on leisure time has increased. Some studies indicate that the absence of leisure time can lead to negative symptoms, and that reasonable amounts of leisure time are important for positive adjustment. Some theorists also believe that leisure time can actually enhance work performance. Overall, the acceptance of leisure time, as a critical consideration in the choice of a career, has increased in recent years.

125. B: "Bandura." The Social Learning Theory of Career Decision-Making, as it was first called by Mitchell and Krumboltz, was later developed into the Learning Theory of Career Counseling (LTCC). Its basic foundation is Albert Bandura's Social Learning Theory as it seeks to explain why people make the choices they do in relation to careers. Some influences on an individual's career choice are environmental conditions, associative learning, and genetic endowment. The LTCC also has the practical application of guiding counselors in dealing the problems that can arise from those choices.

126. A: "environment." The Theory of Work Adjustment (TWA) states that career outcome depends upon satisfaction and satisfactoriness. The former refers to the worker's needs and values in relation to the job, and the latter addresses the worker's skills for the position. How well those two elements fit together impacts the ultimate outcome. Simply stated, both the work environment and the individual must meet each other's needs for the interaction to be maintained, and work adjustment is dependent upon that interaction. How well the requirements of the two factors are met is called correspondence.

127. D: "both A and B." Vocational psychology is concerned with an individual's personality traits as they relate to vocation. It also explores issues such as development over the lifespan, working relationships with others, adaptations to the demands of work, choosing a vocation, and dysfunction. In recent years, interest has also been moving toward global issues. Vocational psychology also develops a variety of assessments (such as job satisfaction and description tests) and methods in relation to personality and vocational choice. Research and methods in vocational psychology are utilized by a variety of professionals, including counseling psychologists.

128. B: "the client who does not enjoy his work." Workaholism is a term that is widely used, but not well defined. It refers to someone who has an overcommitment to work that is not related to external needs. It is generally viewed that there are two types of workaholic, one that likes his work and the other who doesn't like his work. A workaholic who does not like his work is more likely to experience problems as a result. There are also more likely to be problems for the workaholic who has a family-work conflict because of the over-attention to work. This is an increased area of interest in recent years.

129. D: "all of the above." Telecommuting is a recent development in the study of vocational psychology. It is a growing type of work situation that has been brought on by the success of computers and the Internet and the increasing focus on finding a balance between family and work. Telecommuting refers to work that is done in the home setting, rather than at a separate location away from home. There are many advantages for both companies and workers with the telecommuting situation. Some advantages for companies are cost-effectiveness, increased employee retention, and greater productivity. Employees have flexible schedules, more time with family, and are often happier with their jobs.

130. Then answer is C, "occupational stress." Occupational stress refers to stress that is related specifically to the vocational situation. This stress can be affected by issues such as the type of work itself, as well as its relation to the skill set of the individual. It may also relate to the work environment, relationships with coworkers, organizational climate, perceptions and realistic expectations, number of hours worked each week, etc. Research into occupational stress raises questions about its relation to the immune system and general health. This concern is not only significant because of the implications for the individual, but also for society in general (as it increases the cost of health care and loss of productivity for companies).

131. A: "carpenter." John Holland believed that everyone's personality falls into a particular category. He created the Vocational Preference Inventory (VPI), which is a test that measures an individual's particular type and matches it to a career choice that would fit that type. He used a hexagon shape to depict six types of career: realistic, investigative, artistic, social, enterprising, and conventional. Within each type on the hexagon is the variety of actual jobs that would fall into those categories. For example, the "realistic" personality type would include jobs such as a carpenter because it includes people who like to work with tools.

132. B: "males or females." The Minnesota Importance Questionnaire (MIQ) is a useful tool in vocational counseling. The MIQ measures twenty psychological needs and six underlying values as related to work satisfaction, and includes 185 occupations. The six values from which the needs are derived are achievement, comfort, status, autonomy, safety, and altruism. The test is a paper-and-pencil inventory, gender neutral, and appropriate for those who are reading at a fifth-grade level or higher. It can be administered to groups or individuals. A Spanish language edition of the MIQ is also available.

133. C: "measuring the reinforcer characteristics of an occupation." The Minnesota Job Description Questionnaire (MJDQ) is an assessment tool used in vocational counseling. It measures the reinforcer characteristics of a particular job across twenty-one dimensions. There are two forms to the test, one for employees and another for supervisors. Both forms are gender neutral, can be used with both groups or individuals, and are appropriate for those reading at a fifth-grade level or higher. Administration time is approximately twenty minutes. Scoring of the test is best done by a computer program.

134. C: "horns." Rater bias refers to a supervisor's bias in how employees are rated. With the "horns" type of bias, one negative attribute of the employee causes the supervisor to rate everything about that employee more negatively. There are other types of bias also, including leniency, halo, severity, stereotyping, recency, similarity, negative effect, and comparison. Ideally, supervisors will rate their employees in an accurate, realistic manner. However, rater bias can happen, either consciously or unconsciously. When it does happen, it can be costly to both employees and companies, so identifying it, and dealing with it, can be a critical concern.

135. B: "displaced homemaker." A displaced homemaker is someone who has been out of the workforce for a period of time, and is now having difficulty finding suitable employment. The word "homemaker" is used because quite often the displaced homemaker is someone who has left paid employment to run a household or raise children while supported by another relative. Often, displaced homemakers have a variety of marketable skills, but because of the lapse of time since their last paid position, employers are reluctant to hire them. Displaced homemakers may also struggle with feelings of insecurity and inadequacy, which also may make it difficult for them to effectively market themselves.

136. B: "when jobs are contracted outside the company." Outsourcing is when a company takes jobs that would have traditionally been done in-house, and contracts with another company to have them done from somewhere else. Companies increasingly outsource jobs because it can save them money in overhead expenses and benefits, and it usually costs less to get the job done than if they did it with an in-house employee. Outsourcing can also save in time for management as the outsourced jobs are managed by the contracted company. Disadvantages to the company are control and communication. For the employee, outsourcing can be viewed as negative if one's job is eliminated because of it or positive if one is with the contracted company.

137. A: "rationalization." Rationalization is a Freudian psychoanalytic defense mechanism. It occurs when the ego rejects the real motive for the individual's behavior and substitutes it with a motive that will make the behavior seem more acceptable. A client is likely to feel anxiety when acting in a manner that, for whatever reason, runs counter to what he believes is right. In order to make himself feel better for his behavior, the client will come up with reasons for his behavior (in an effort to make it seem more acceptable), and thus reduce his overall anxiety level.

138. B: "a way to experience the world as your client does." Empathy is a critical tool in counseling because it assists the counselor in understanding the internal workings of the client's mind. It's important to note that the term "empathy" (when used in relation to therapy), does not have the same meaning as it does in general use. Empathy does not refer to feeling the same feelings as the client, or having sympathy for the client. Rather, it's a way to experience the world as the client does, and thus gain a deeper understanding of the client's thoughts and feelings.

139. D: "all of the above." There are several criticisms of Rogerian therapy. One common criticism is that while Carl Rogers does take the unconscious into account in his writings, he doesn't give it enough emphasis. Likewise, Rogers doesn't incorporate information relative to developmental stages into his therapy. Rogers is also sometimes criticized because his therapeutic method is not appropriate for use with some types of mental illness. For example, some individuals may not have the ability for self-expression, or feel anxiety for their actions. Rogers' theory also assumes that people are basically good and healthy, so application with clients who are particularly violent or lacking in personal or social conscience may be difficult.

140. A: "to remove the hierarchical element between client and therapist." Carl Rogers believed that therapy should involve a warm, close, and positive relationship between client and therapist. He also believed that the therapeutic environment should likewise be a very positive and supportive one. He used the term "client" instead of "patient" because he wanted to eliminate the hierarchical relationship that was more traditional between patient and client, and instead encourage a feeling of equals. The terminology fits well with the overall emphasis on the client directing the therapy and the therapist acting more as a guide in that process.

141. D: "Gestalt therapy." Frederick and Laura Perls developed Gestalt therapy. Its focus is on challenging clients to become more self-aware and face their problems. Frederick Perls was a student of psychoanalysis, and trained as a Freudian psychoanalyst. As such, he believed that many problems resulted from early conflicts. However, he also believed that those conflicts should be forced into the here and now for clients to deal with. He believed that counselors should confront clients with questions that would lead them to face their thoughts and feelings, and force them to choose if they will allow the past to control the present.

142. C: "Gestalt." One of the techniques of Gestalt therapy is role playing. Since Gestalt therapy stresses the importance of facing feelings, role playing is an effective way to explore and express feelings toward another without their actual presence. In role playing, the counselor acts the part of someone the client is in conflict with, providing the client with the opportunity to say and do what they would want to if the person were really present. Sometimes the roles will be reversed in role playing as well, depending upon the needs of the situation. Role playing is a way to deal with feelings in a positive manner, with an ultimate goal of ensuring that feelings do not control the individual.

143. B: "thoughts and feelings." A basic idea of cognitive-behavioral therapy is that we can't change the world around us or many of the events that occur in our lives, but we can change how we think and feel about everything. In cognitive-behavioral theory, our thoughts cause our feelings and behaviors. Since thoughts can be faulty, they can cause us to feel, and choose behaviors, that are problematic. By changing inappropriate thoughts, we can change how we think and feel about situations, and also how we choose to behave in response to those situations, even when we can't change the situations themselves.

144. C: "rational-emotive therapy." Albert Ellis developed rational emotive therapy (RET) in the mid-1950s. He believed that, in many cases, people are unhappy, and choose negative behaviors because of irrational thought processes. He felt there were three types of unrealistic views: people feel they must perform well to be approved of by others, must be treated fairly by others, and must have things go their way...or they will be unhappy. The RET therapist works to change irrational beliefs and promote rational self-talk. The therapist will challenge irrational thoughts and even assign homework to aid in combating irrational thinking and promote positive thoughts, feelings, and behaviors.

145. B: "Humanistic." Humanistic psychology is often known as the "third force" in psychology because it came after psychoanalytic theory and behaviorism. Its founders are usually identified as Rollo May, Abraham Maslow, and Carl Rogers. It is also viewed as having its roots in existentialist thought, because it addresses not just illness, but the meaning of human existence. Humanistic psychology defined itself as different from psychoanalysis and behaviorism by its focus on helping the individual to achieve full potential. Psychoanalysis and behaviorism focused on problems and the elimination of those problems in the individual, but humanistic psychology moved beyond that to do more than simply alleviate problems and focus on the healthy aspects of the individual.

146. A: "Rogerian therapist." It is the Rogerian therapist who is more likely to establish a rapport the quickest with the client. The Rogerian therapist is warm and inviting, communicating to the client respect and the feeling of control. By contrast, the Freudian therapist is more likely to seem analytical and somewhat distant. Rational-emotive and Gestalt therapists are confrontational in their therapeutic approach, which may make the client feel less inclined toward a strong rapport at an earlier stage. Rogerian therapists don't force entry into the unconscious or confront or contradict the client. They simply mirror back what they see in the client, and guide them to an independent and self-directed state. This approach would certainly appeal to many clients, and be more likely to encourage a swift and positive rapport between client and therapist.

147. D: "Gestalt." Gestalt theory, developed by Frederick and Laura Perls, lists "reflection" as a defense mechanism. Reflection in Gestalt therapy, put simply, is doing to oneself what one wishes to do to someone else. Sometimes that can be something obvious, such as a man cutting his own arm when he really wants to act out aggressively toward someone else. At other times, the reflection may be less apparent, such as a young woman feeling resentment toward a friend, but turning that toward herself as depressive feelings instead. Reflection can become pathological when it's chronic, but often exists in a healthy personality.

148. D: "both A and C." Systematic desensitization is a type of classical conditioning. It's a behavioral therapy used to treat anxiety with relaxation and repeated exposure to the anxiety-producing situation. A common example would be a client who has a fear of spiders. The counselor teaches the client relaxation techniques, and systematically brings the client closer and closer to a spider. At each step, the client achieves relaxation before moving on. Eventually, the client is able to be in the presence of a spider without excessive anxiety. Systematic desensitization can be achieved utilizing imagery as well, and is considered an effective therapy, especially for phobias.

149. D: "aversive conditioning." Aversive conditioning is a classical conditioning approach. Behavioral therapists use aversive conditioning to pair negative stimuli with the behavior that needs to be changed. The idea is for the reward value of the unwanted behavior to be eliminated, so that the client will no longer choose to engage in it. A common example for aversive conditioning is a client who has a drinking problem. The counselor may recommend medication that induces nausea when alcohol is consumed. The negative experience of nausea when drinking replaces the pleasurable experience of drinking, which eventually may result in the client choosing to stop drinking altogether.

150. D: "all of the above." The basic idea behind operant conditioning is that the consequences of behaviors have an effect on the individual's choice to engage in those behaviors. There are four types of operant conditioning, two of which weaken behaviors, and two of which can strengthen it. Punishment is one type of operant conditioning that weakens the behavior. Put simply, it involves giving a negative consequence every time the behavior occurs. For example, a client who wishes to stop swearing may snap a rubber band on his wrist whenever he swears. The sharp, uncomfortable sensation of the snap, as

- 63 -

well as the embarrassment of snapping the wrist in public, pairs a negative consequence with the behavior of swearing. The negative consequence may cause the unwanted behavior to eventually cease.

151. B: "positive reinforcement." Positive reinforcement is a type of operant conditioning used in behavioral therapy. It's a way in which to strengthen a desirable behavior. An example of positive reinforcement would be if you wanted a dog to sit upon command. Every time the dog successfully sits when given the command to do so, the dog would be rewarded with a positive consequence (such as a dog treat or pat on the head). Eventually the dog would come to identify the positive reinforcement with the behavior of sitting upon command, and therefore continue the wanted behavior on a consistent basis.

152. B: "Eric Berne." Eric Berne is a psychologist who formulated a "life script" theory that addresses personality development and interpersonal relationships. The theory states that people form a life script early in their childhood years that sets the stage for how their future will develop. Individuals make decisions in their early life to live their life in a particular way as a means to ensure survival (based upon a number of considerations such as parental, social, and cultural). Transactional analysis (TA) is a psychotherapy used to make changes to an individual's life script in order for a happier, healthier life to develop.

153. C: "skills acquisition." Donald Meichenbaum's stress inoculation training (SIT) was developed to help individuals cope with the aftermath of stressful events, and also to serve to "inoculate" people against future stressful reactions. There are three stages to SIT. In the initial "conceptualization" stage, the focus is on the relationship between client and counselor. "Skill acquisition" and "rehearsal" are the focus of the second stage of SIT, which teaches coping skills to the client. The third stage of "application" and "follow through" deals with, as stated, the application of the techniques learned. SIT can be conducted with individuals, couples, or groups.

154. C: "bibliotherapy." Bibliotherapy is just as it sounds, a type of therapy that uses reading material to enhance the therapeutic experience. Bibliotherapy often involves the simple assignment of reading material that would be meaningful to the client and the direction the therapy is taking. However, it can also include activities and exercises related to the reading assignment. The use of bibliotherapy has various applications, depending upon the client, symptoms, and treatment being used. It can be a time-saving method used to significantly advance the course of therapy. Some people also view bibliotherapy as a self-help technique when not used in the traditional therapeutic setting.

155. A: "REBT." Rational-Emotive Behavior Therapy (REBT), by Albert Ellis, deals not only with behaviors and feelings, but also with the thoughts behind them. Irrational ideas are believed to be the basic reason for the unpleasant and/or unwanted feelings and behaviors of a client. Ellis theorized that there are twelve core irrational beliefs that can cause or sustain psychological difficulties. One of those core beliefs is that the significant others of an individual must love them for nearly anything they do, instead of the healthier focus on self-respect and loving others without expectation of love being returned.

156. A: "freedom." In William Glasser's choice theory (renamed from "control theory"), there are five fundamental psychological needs. "Survival" is the first, which is paid little attention to unless threatened. "Love and Belonging" is next, indicating that we, as humans, all have a basic need for acceptance. The third stage is for "Power/Recognition," referring to the individual goals that people have, and the need to achieve those goals on some level. "Freedom" comes fourth, and ties into our sense of fair play and need to have a choice in our lives. Finally, the last fundamental psychological need is for "fun," which is the ultimate goal for pleasure.

157. D: "William Glasser." William Glasser's choice theory states that all behavior consists of either "what we do," "what we think," or "what we feel." He theorized that one can only control one's own behavior, and that every behavior chosen is an attempt to meet one's internal needs at the time. Unlike the stimulus-response theories that are popular for controlling behavior and encouraging change, Glasser believed that only the individual can control himself, and it's not possible to do so with reinforcements or other such inducements. He further theorized that for people to be happy with their lives, they need to find ways to meet their inner needs.

158. A: "silence." Silence is often difficult for anyone in a social setting, but it can be particularly troublesome for a counselor and client in the therapeutic setting when not properly understood. Society in general often views silence as a sign of disinterest, rudeness, or awkwardness. In therapy, however, silence can take on another meaning. Silence is not always best used with very disturbed clients. However, it can be a valuable tool for general use. Silence not only is a means to convey empathy and understanding at particular moments, but is also a means by which to encourage deeper thought and retrospection. It can also apply subtle pressure upon the client who is resistant or otherwise holding back.

159. D: "self-efficacy." Self-efficacy is the belief that one can overcome obstacles. Self-efficacy is a factor in cognitive-behavior therapy, which seeks to change the client's thoughts in an effort to also change the client's behavior. Bandura believed that self-efficacy was very important if therapy was to be successful. By telling oneself messages such as "I can do this," self-confidence is enhanced and eventually the client puts increased effort forth to solve problems, which eliminates many long-term difficulties. Constructive self-talk is also often used in cognitive-behavior therapy, which aids in the development of self-efficacy.

160. A: "behavior that is maladaptive and harmful." What is normal (or abnormal) can certainly be debated, but in psychology, "abnormal" behavior is generally viewed as behavior that is maladaptive and harmful. If the behavior is harmful to the self or others and/or causing significant difficulties in the individual's life, then the behavior may be termed abnormal. In the medical model, abnormality is due to an illness, but psychology takes a broader view than this. The Diagnostic and Statistical Manual of Mental Disorders (DSM), published by the American Psychiatric Association, contains definitions and

- 65 -

classifications of mental disorders, which aids in the determination of what is to be considered "normal."

161. B: "its unconscious material." In Freudian psychoanalysis, dream analysis is a psychotherapeutic technique used to interpret the client's dreams. Freud believed that dreams contain information about unconscious thoughts and conflicts that can be useful in treating the client. "Manifest content" is the term given for the conscious (or remembered) parts of the dream. "Latent content" is unconscious (not remembered) material from the dream. Psychoanalysts analyze the manifest content (in an attempt to get at the latent content) as a way to better understand the inner workings of the client's mind, especially material that might be sexual or aggressive in nature.

162. A: "a behavioral modification technique." A "token economy" is a behavior modification technique. Tokens (a tangible, material item) are given to the client when target behaviors occur. The client can later turn his tokens in for something of a more significant value. This modification method is useful in settings such as mental hospitals and school classrooms. It has been sometimes criticized for creating a system in which the clients are too attached to the token system, and once the system is ended, the positive effects also cease to exist. This operant conditioning approach has the ultimate goal of seeing the positive behavior continue even after the token system is eventually eliminated.

163. C: "cognitive." Behavior therapies focus on eliminating or changing the client's undesirable behavior, unlike psychoanalysts who focus on unconscious thoughts and the origins of the reasons behind behaviors. In order to investigate abnormal behaviors, cognitive therapists emphasize the client's thoughts. They believe that if the client's thoughts and feelings change, then so will the unwanted behavior. Cognitive therapists are more conversational in their approach than cognitive-behavioral therapists, who use a lot of exercises and training sessions. The cognitive approach seems more traditional than the cognitive-behavioral approach.

164. C: "human will." Logotherapy, developed by Viktor Frankl, is an existential psychology that focuses on the search for meaning. The human spirit plays an integral role in Logotherapy, which is more about the human will or spirit, rather than related to religion or a relationship with God. Frankl taught that everything can be taken away from us in life, except for our will to find meaning in our lives. Logotherapy seeks to aid individuals in overcoming obstacles with the power of the human spirit. Frankl theorized that we can find meaning in our lives through deeds, by experiencing a value, or through suffering.

165. D: "all of the above." Novice counselors sometimes experience difficulty in facilitating conversation with their clients. This problem is often due to an excess of pointed questions that do not allow for the client to expand upon the inquiry. Open-ended questions are far more productive, and urge the client to expound upon the subject matter raised. Restatement of the client's comments (as in a Rogerian approach) can also stimulate further discussion on the part of the client, as can silence, which often has an unspoken expectation of the client's response. Time and experience usually alleviate this problem

with novice counselors as they become more comfortable with the counseling situation and their professional skills.

166. D: "both B and C." B. F. Skinner believed that behavior is determined from external factors rather than from internal issues. He theorized that reinforcements can be used to control behavior, and that punishment was one of the ways that behavior could be modified. However, Skinner believed that punishment was not the best technique for behavior modification. He felt that an individual will work harder, and learn faster, when positive reinforcement is used. He theorized that there are many alternatives to the use of punishment as a reinforcer, and that those options should take precedence when possible.

167. C: "Premack Principle." Premack's Principle of reinforcement was developed by David Premack in 1965 out of a study completed with monkeys. It states that high-probability behaviors (HPB) will reinforce low-probability behaviors (LPB). In the case of this question, your client doesn't like to shower and dress well. However, he is willing to do so because of the attention it gives him from a girl he likes. In other words, he is willing to engage in behavior he doesn't like in order to get something that he does. The Premack Principle has a variety of uses, included its use in animal training.

168. B: "antidepressant." Tricyclic drugs are called antidepressant drugs because they regulate mood. They are called "tricyclic" because of their three-ringed molecular structure. They can correct chemical imbalances in the brain, and raise the levels of serotonin and norepinephrine. Tricyclic drugs are available in several forms, including, pills, liquid, and injection. Some commonly used antidepressants are amitriptyline, nortriptyline, and protriptyline. Depending upon the particular drug used, side effects can include dizziness, bladder problems, dry mouth, and an increased heart rate, among other issues. It takes some time for the medication to work, so several weeks should be allowed before deciding if the medication is having its desired effect.

169. B: "involves little discomfort." Electroconvulsive therapy (ECT), also known as "shock treatment," is often thought of as a controversial treatment. However, ECT has been found to be effective with some patients, and especially those with severe depression. ECT was developed in 1938, and because of the stigma associated with it in the 1960s, its practice declined. In ECT, two small electrodes are placed on the patient's head and administer a small electrical current. The current causes a seizure that lasts less than one minute. Contrary to popular belief, ECT is not significantly painful and in some cases patients can even sleep through it.

170. A: "a last resort treatment." Psychosurgery refers to surgery that removes or destroys brain tissue in order to improve a mental health condition. Egas Moniz developed the "prefrontal lobotomy" to surgically sever the frontal lobe. He believed that severe mental illnesses could be alleviated by this surgery. Moniz was awarded the Nobel Prize in 1949 for his work, but since prefrontal lobotomies often leave patients in a vegetative state, this treatment is no longer used. Today psychosurgery is considered a last resort, and performed in a far more precise manner.

171. D: "resistance." Hans Selye, a researcher on stress, developed the general adaptation syndrome (GAS) to explain the effects of stress upon the human body. The body first enters into a state of shock in the "alarm stage." Blood pressure drops, decreased temperature, and lost muscle tone are a few of the symptoms of this stage. Stage two is called the "resistance stage," when such things as stress hormones, heart rate, and respiration all increase. If the body is unable to eliminate the stress, the third stage of "exhaustion" begins. In this final stage, the individual may be more susceptible to illness or even collapse.

172. D: "both B and C." Richard Lazarus theorized that there were two forms of coping. One type, called "problem-focused coping," is utilized by individuals who face their difficulties directly and try to solve them. This is a more direct approach, facing issues head-on. By contrast, "emotion-focused coping" is used by people who are more likely to avoid their problems, pray for help, rationalize, or use other defense mechanisms. Emotion-focused coping can be productive in times when a delay in dealing with stress is the best course of action; however, overall, problem-focused coping is usually the best strategy.

173. B: "biofeedback." Biofeedback is a means to measure involuntary physiological behaviors and report them to the client. It grew out of an interest in the mind-body connection, and has been shown to be quite useful in some cases. By using cognitive-control methods, clients can learn to control physiological responses, and therefore manage such things as chronic pain, irritable bowel syndrome (IBS), high blood pressure, and headaches. It is also often used with stress-related issues such as depression, anxiety, and sleep disorders, and is being used with some psychiatric disorders as well. Because biofeedback can sometimes be used to voluntarily control involuntary (automatic physical) responses, its potential is significant.

174. D: "four." William Masters and Virginia Johnson studied the physiological responses of hundreds of subjects to determine that there are four phases of sexual response. The first phase is "excitement" and lasts from minutes to hours. During this phase there is increased genital blood flow and muscle tension. "Plateau" is the next phase and consists of such responses as increased pulse rate, rapid breathing, and raised blood pressure. The third phase of "orgasm" brings intense pleasure and extreme completion of neuromuscular tension. The human sexual response concludes with the fourth stage of "resolution" with the arousal dropping off, and the return to a normal resting state.

175. C: "under moderate levels of arousal." The Yerkes-Dodson law says that people tend to perform best under moderate levels of arousal. If arousal is too high for an individual, it may be difficult to maintain focus on a particular duty or activity. Too low an arousal level, and the individual may not feel motivated enough to complete a job, or lack the necessary energy to perform a given task. Of course, the optimal level of arousal for maximum productivity differs from person-to-person. For example, one person's high arousal may seem like moderate arousal to another. However, overall, moderate levels of arousal tend to be best for optimal performance.

176. B: "emotion precedes a physiological response." The James-Lange theory of Emotion was proposed in 1884, and is a combination of the ideas of William James and Carl Lange. The theory states that one's body reacts to a stimulus first, and is then followed by the emotional reaction. For example, a spider lands on an individual's arm. The individual jumps and screams in reaction. The individual then interprets the body's reaction as fear, thus leading to actually feeling the emotion of fearfulness. This idea of the physiological response preceding the emotional one was new at the time, and one of the first theories used to explain the science of emotion.

177. B: "Freud." A narcissistic client is only interested in issues related to self. His body, thoughts, needs, and anything that is related to him is what seems real. Everything else, as not related to the self, is not perceived as real or of interest by the narcissistic personality. This issue was discussed early in psychology theory. Freud talked about "primary narcissism" as a time when, as infants, individuals are unable to differentiate between self and others. Self-interest is not without its positive aspects, however, as it can be useful in the interest of self-preservation. However, a pathological narcissism can interfere with interpersonal relationships and social connectedness, leading to further problems in the client's life.

178. D: "all of the above." Erich Fromm believed that family, politics, or any other form of authoritative power can destroy an individual's potential. He had similar concerns about religion. Erich Fromm felt that religious faith and experience was fine. He didn't take a stand against religious belief in and of itself, but rather had concerns about some aspects of it, and its possible negative effects. He believed that religious tenets could be used to encourage divisiveness and warfare, and that some principles were misdated and misguided (which could possibly lead to harmful choices). He didn't like the authoritarian value system, and focused on the need for individuals to use reason and independent thought in making decisions.

179. A: "tension." Harry Stack Sullivan theorized that "euphoria" occurs in the absence of internal "tension," and tension manifests itself as the opposite extreme. There are four types of tension, with biological needs (such as the need for food and water) causing the first type of tension. Sleep is not included in Sullivan's first type of tension, because he considers it a separate type of need, deserving of its own "type." Perhaps the most critical of the types of tension is the third, "anxiety." Anxiety can be caused in various ways and exist on a variety of levels, depending upon the individual situation. The final type of tension is related to "fear."

180. A: "Sigmund Freud." Erik Erikson essentially supports much of Sigmund Freud's theory, but is more socially and culturally oriented than Sigmund Freud was. Erikson extended beyond Freud's theory of development, theorizing eight separate psychological struggles that are critical to the development of the personality. He believed that there is evidence from as far back as primitive cultures of a belief in the unconscious. That's one of the reasons he felt one of Freud's greatest contributions to psychology was the idea of the unconscious and its role in the lives of individuals.

181. A: "Allport." An irrational hostility toward another that is merely due to that individual's membership in a particular group is how Gordon Allport would define "prejudice." Allport believed that prejudice was a complex issue and caused by a variety of factors. He points out that the nature of prejudice is such that it can't be affected by the addition of rational facts. Situational issues such as economic factors, cultural factors, advertising, historical issues, and stereotyping are just a few of the possible influences upon the development of prejudice. Allport believed that prejudice should be regarded as a type of psychopathology, as it leads to such things as the increased use of defense mechanisms, passivity, and withdrawal.

182. A: "corollaries." George Kelly believed that each individual has an underlying "fundamental postulate" that affects everything else. In his theory, eleven corollaries help to define one's personal constructs. The corollaries include the following: "Construction," which basically says we base our expectations on past experiences. "Individuality" says that everyone interprets things differently. "Organization" refers to every person's organization of constructs into a hierarchy. Each person's construct is bipolar, so that's how "Dichotomy" could be described, while "Choice" is as it sounds. "Range," "Experience," Modulation," "Fragmentation," "Commonality," and "Sociality" round out the rest of the eleven.

183. A: "source, surface, and unique." To Raymond Cattell, personality is about being able to predict an individual's behavior in any given situation. Part of this is an understanding that the components of an individual's personality are made up of "source traits," which one can only identify through "factor analysis." This is not to be confused with "surface traits" that are personality characteristics resulting from two or more source traits. Surface traits are not a basic component of personality. Also not to be confused is the term "unique trait," which simply refers to a trait that is unique to an individual and not shared by others.

184. D: "antianxiety." Antianxiety drugs are also sometimes called tranquilizers or benzodiazepines. They work by affecting the central nervous system, and have an overall calming effect on the client. They tend to be fast-acting, so can be useful for times of panic as well as for long-term anxiety issues. These medications work quite well for many clients, but there can be some negative side effects. Sleepiness, dizziness, and other such sedative-related side effects can make it difficult for some clients to effectively conduct their daily lives while medicated. Some commonly prescribed anti-anxiety drugs are alprazolam, diazepam, and lorazepam.

185. B: "antipsychotic." Antipsychotic (or neuroleptic) medications have been in use since the 1950s, and are quite effective overall for schizophrenia. These medications work by affecting neurotransmitters in the brain. They are not, however, a cure-all. The need for medication is highly individualized and may or may not work depending upon the situation. Some patients are helped a great deal, but for others the medications aren't effective. Antipsychotic drugs are often particularly helpful with delusions and hallucinations. Reported side effects include weight gain, drowsiness, muscle spasms,

fidgeting, shaking, or stiffness, and sometimes heart problems. Commonly prescribed antipsychotic medications are quetiapine, chlorpromazine, and aripiprazole.

186. B: "a deep state of relaxation." Hypnosis may be best described as a deep state of relaxation. It is during this relaxed state that the mind is quieted and open to suggestion. Franz Mesmer (the "father of hypnosis") is credited with developing the technique, but it wasn't called "hypnosis" until the 1800s when James Braid experimented with trance-like states on patients. Jean-Martin Charcot used hypnosis successfully to treat hysterics, and Sigmund Freud used hypnosis in his work as well. Hypnosis is sometimes vilified as nothing more than a parlor trick, but, in reality, it can be highly effective in therapeutic settings when conducted by a trained hypnotherapist.

187. D: "all of the above." Hypnosis is, simply put, a deep state of relaxation in which the client is not quite awake and not quite asleep. It is a trance-like, in-between state. During this state, the client is more open to suggestion and sometimes better able to utilize recall of various events. Many people believe that hypnosis is only a magician's trick, or if legitimate at all, useful only for memory recall or psychological issues. However, hypnosis is often used today to treat such medical issues as asthma, chronic pain, easing childbirth, lowering blood pressure, and many others.

188. B: "many, not." Millions of men suffer from depression each year, yet relatively few are likely to seek help for it. Instead of enlisting the aid of a medical professional, men often self-medicate with drugs or alcohol, which merely masks the symptoms rather than addressing them. Furthermore, depression in men is often overlooked because their symptoms are sometimes not what is expected of a depressed individual. Instead of the typical sadness, male depressive symptoms are often such things as irritability, anger, and aggressive acting-out. Attention to older men is also needed because illness and medications can mask depressive symptoms and cause elderly men to be less likely to receive help.

189. B: "contingencies of reinforcement." B.F. Skinner called his "Skinner box" an operant conditioning apparatus. There are various versions of the box, but one type consists of a small box that is soundproof with a lighted disk or bar at one end that releases food when manipulated by the subject. Skinner used his Skinner boxes with different animals, including pigeons and rats. Sometimes the disk or bar would be positioned differently, or have various colors, depending upon the needs of the experiment. The disk might also be electrified, for studying negative reinforcement. The purpose of the Skinner box was to study the "contingencies of reinforcement" that B.F. Skinner believed control behavior, which include the interrelationships between stimuli, response, and the consequences of those responses.

190. B: "increase." B.F. Skinner found that deprivation will increase the probability of an operant. For example, a rat deprived of food for some time is far more likely to press a bar to receive food than a rat that has not been deprived of food. B.F. Skinner would view the rat's hunger, not as an internal process, but rather as an external, measurable one (ie, the

amount of time without food). Just as deprivation will increase an operant, satiation will decrease it. For instance, a rat that has been given his fill of food and water is much less likely to manipulate a bar in order to receive food.

191. A: "an example of behavioral control through conditioning." B.F. Skinner, as a behaviorist, attributed all behavior to external (rather than internal) causes. He would likely have viewed religious belief as a result of early parental conditioning. Skinner would have believed that religion gains control by attributing power to some supernatural force that punishes unacceptable behaviors (ie, hell) and rewards desired behaviors (ie, heaven). He did not believe that an individual had faith in a particular religion because of inner reasons, but rather simply because of the external reinforcements of the religion, such as parents and society.

192. C: "cognition." Albert Bandura believed that behavior and reinforcement did not always have to take place for learning to occur. He believed that "modeling" (or learning just by seeing someone else do something) was a significant type of learning. If one could only learn by trial and error, the cost of errors could be too costly and so modeling is a far more reasonable way to learn. Bandura also theorized that observational learning happens through cognition. Imagining oneself in the same situation as someone else causes the modeling to successfully occur. Because of its cognitive nature, there's a lot of opportunity for creativity with modeling as well. As the individual imagines himself in the same situation; he may combine more than one situation to attain learning of it, thus producing a more creative process.

193. D: "female sexuality." While all of Sigmund Freud's theories have been criticized over the years, his view of female sexuality would be the most controversial. Freud worked in therapy with many female patients, and came to believe that females are weaker than males and certainly inferior in many other ways as well. For example, he believed that female sexual organs were inferior and that clitoral orgasm was an immature response. Superego development in females was also viewed as weak, and he considered females for more susceptible to neurotic behavior.

194. A: "goals." Carl Jung believed that one's personality is not merely a product of the past, but also shaped by the present and future. He viewed personality as something that evolves over time. Jung theorized that an individual's behavior must be analyzed with its teleology (goals) in mind. He saw teleology as a process external to humans as well as a method for inquiry. For this reason, he diverted from Freud's focus on the past and its effects on the personality to theorize that all behavior will be understood by a combination of past, one's attempt to grow, and future orientation, rather than the past alone.

195. A: "is formed at birth." Carl Jung's idea of the "personal unconscious" is something that forms just after birth, and consists of experience that the individual is not aware of. Some memories are forgotten and others easily recalled. Some memories may be repressed for various reasons, and others may be subliminal (beyond our sensory awareness) in nature. Whatever the reasons, however, the personal unconscious consists of material from one's

thoughts and experiences that slip out of consciousness to become unconscious. It's also important to note that Jung believed that awareness of the personal unconscious was necessary for one to further the goal of self-awareness.

196. B: "to bring unconscious material into the conscious." Free Association is a fundamental rule of psychoanalysis, and meant to bring unconscious material into conscious awareness. Free Association differs from usual conversation. In social conversation, an individual carefully chooses what he will say, selecting material that will fit the conversation, or that is appropriate to the circumstances. In Free Association, the patient is encouraged to say whatever comes into his mind, no matter how silly or inappropriate it may be. The therapist carefully attends to what is being said, analyzing the content and bringing the unconscious forward.

197. D: "all of the above." Regression is a defense mechanism theorized by Sigmund Freud. Freud believed that some people, when confronted with high levels of stress, may regress to a prior time in their lives when they felt safe and protected. Many times this regression may be to an earlier psychosexual stage in which the patient is now fixated. For example, an individual who was fixated at the oral stage may regress to sucking his thumb when faced with the extreme stress of a terminal illness diagnosis. The defense mechanism works for the patient because the thumb-sucking reduces the patient's stressful feelings.

198. A: "Superego." According to Freudian psychoanalytic theory, the conscience resides in the Superego. The Id knows only what the individual wants; the Ego knows it can't always get what it wants and negotiates between the Id and the Superego. The Superego is the moral part of the mind, imposing rules and punishing inappropriate thoughts and actions. For this reason, the Superego (where the conscience is) causes the Ego to feel anxiety/guilt when the individual's behavior diverts from what is deemed morally acceptable. The Superego is an important part of the personality for obvious reasons. If the Superego is underdeveloped, the individual may not experience the necessary tension between the Ego and Superego, and thus act inappropriately in interpersonal relationships or in society in general.

199. C: "a Freudian slip." A Freudian slip has become a popular part of everyday conversation, and refers to the idea that what seems to be accidental may actually provide a window into the unconscious, and what one really thinks and feels. Many people believe that a Freudian slip is only an errant verbal comment, but such a slip can be anything, including physical acts that are caused by the unconscious part of the personality. Freud believed that such slips reveal an unconscious thought, belief, or wish that is sometimes held from conscious thought because it would be deemed unacceptable in some way.

200. B: "first born." Alfred Adler's birth order theory rejects the idea that children born within the same family, and raised within similar circumstances, are unaffected by the order in which they were born. He believed that one could make determinations about the personality of an individual simply by where in the family birth order the child was placed. For example, the firstborn often suffers from feelings of inferiority because of being

dethroned from his place of total attentiveness by subsequent children. The firstborn works hard to follow in his parent's footsteps and embraces responsibility.

Practice Test #2

Practice Questions

1. Susie is playing with blocks and is trying to build a tower; she tries but cannot build a tower. Susie's mother helps her build a four-block tower. Later, Susie builds a four-block tower without her mother's help. According to Vygotsky, the inability to build the tower on her own is known as:
   a. scaffolding
   b. the zone of proximal development
   c. assisted discovery
   d. learning by imitation

2. According to Erickson, when an individual fails to develop a strong sense of identity, the individual will have troubles with the development of:
   a. autonomy
   b. initiative
   c. intimacy
   d. integrity

3. Which of the following is the correct sequence of stages in Freud's theory of personality development?
   a. Oral, genital, latency, anal, phallic
   b. Genital, anal, phallic, oral, latency
   c. Latency, phallic, oral, anal, genital
   d. Oral, anal, phallic, latency, genital

4. Jacob's father tells Jacob to clean his room. When Jacob asks why, his father responds, "Because I said so." The father's response is most representative of which parenting style?
   a. Uninvolved
   b. Authoritarian
   c. Authoritative
   d. Permissive

5. Harry Harlow used baby monkeys and several different kinds of "surrogate mothers" to investigate which factors are important in early development and attachment. According to his findings, baby monkeys:
   a. preferred a soft terrycloth "mother" to a wire-mesh "mother" that held a bottle
   b. preferred a wire-mesh "mother" that held a bottle to a soft terrycloth "mother"
   c. showed no preference
   d. preferred neither "mother"

6. Which of the following is a myth about suicide in the United States?
    a. Male suicide is four times higher than that among females.
    b. It occurs in age groups of 90 years and up.
    c. Psychiatrists, physicians, and dentists are most prone.
    d. Asking someone about suicide may push that person over the edge.

7. Cody does what his parents say because he doesn't want to lose his television privileges. This is an example of what level in Kohlberg's theory of moral development?
    a. Integrity versus despair
    b. Preconventional
    c. Conventional
    d. Postconventional

8. Josie likes to play peek-a-boo with her little brother, Jack. According to Piaget, Jack finds this game fun because he has acquired _____, which is one of the primary tasks of the sensorimotor stage of cognitive development.
    a. conservation
    b. dual representation
    c. object permanence
    d. reversibility

9. The theorist associated with bonding and attachment is:
    a. Bowlby
    b. Adler
    c. Freud
    d. Piaget

10. Henry, a 72-year-old widower, reminisces with his daughter about his life. He talks about his successes and regrets. This is an example of Erikson's:
    a. intimacy stage
    b. generativity stage
    c. industry stage
    d. ego integrity stage

11. When it comes to displaying aggression, girls more often engage in _____ aggression than boys.
    a. hostile
    b. instrumental
    c. relational
    d. physical

- 76 -

12. All of the following are physical characteristics of Down Syndrome EXCEPT:
    a. short, stocky build
    b. almond-shaped eyes
    c. large hands and feet
    d. flattened face

13. Which of the following statements is true when considering cultural and familial influences on self-esteem?
    a. Chinese and Japanese children have higher self-esteem than North American children, mainly because their cultures have higher academic standards for achievement.
    b. Boys tend to have lower self-esteem than girls.
    c. African American children tend to have lower self-esteem than Caucasian children.
    d. An authoritative parenting style usually allows children to have especially high self-esteem.

14. Research on gay and lesbian parents indicates:
    a. Their children are maladjusted.
    b. They are as dedicated to and effective at child rearing as are heterosexual parents.
    c. They are less dedicated to child rearing than heterosexual parents.
    d. Their children are parented harshly and inconsistently.

15. In the Stanford prison study, what caused the guards to treat the prisoners harshly?
    a. Their instructions from the researchers
    b. The uncooperative behavior of the prisoners
    c. The social context
    d. The pressure the guards got from one another

16. In the original studies, Milgram and his colleagues found that people were more likely to disobey under all of the following circumstances EXCEPT when _____.
    a. the victim was in an adjoining room so the "teacher" heard every sound the victim made
    b. two experimenters had conflicting demands about the continuation of the experiment
    c. the person ordering them to continue was an ordinary man, apparently another volunteer
    d. the subject worked with peers who refused to go further in the procedure

17. In the Stanford prison simulation, male college students agreed to participate in an experiment to discover what would happen when they took on the roles of prisoners and guards. The researchers found that _____.
    a. within a short time the prisoners became distressed and panicky, with accompanying emotional and physical ailments
    b. a small percentage of the guards became tyrannical and abusive in order to maintain the social structure of the prison
    c. the "tough but fair" guards urged the tyrannical guards to lighten up on the prisoners
    d. all of the prisoners and the guards became harsh and abusive

- 77 -

18. In what ways do stereotypes distort reality?
   a. Stereotypes exaggerate the differences that exist between groups.
   b. Stereotypes exaggerate the differences that exist within groups.
   c. Stereotypes produce many differing perceptions by many people.
   d. Stereotypes demonstrate that members of a group can be different.

19. Jennifer has to choose between spending the evening at home with her parents or spending the evening babysitting her younger sister. Jennifer does not like either of these choices. This situation describes an:
   a. approach-avoidance conflict
   b. avoidance-avoidance conflict
   c. approach-approach conflict
   d. avoidance vector

20. Connie tells each of her clients that the best way she can help them is to attempt to look at the world from the client's point of view. This counselor is taking the _____ perspective.
   a. etic
   b. alloplastic
   c. emic
   d. autoplastic

21. Working with individuals from different cultures requires that the counselor:
   a. have sensitivity to the needs of the individuals
   b. make a referral to another counselor
   c. have knowledge about the different cultures
   d. Both A and C.

22. A high standard of counseling practice when working with diverse populations involves all of the following EXCEPT:
   a. treating all clients the same way
   b. acknowledging and confronting their own biases and prejudices
   c. adapting one's knowledge and skills to meet the clients' needs
   d. educating oneself as completely as possible regarding the clients' cultural context

23. When working with individuals from different cultures, the effective counselor may not:
   a. use language similar to the client's
   b. maintain good eye contact at all times
   c. be cognizant of the context
   d. honor religious beliefs

24. Murray is a bright student, but he procrastinates. He puts off writing term papers and gets incompletes, which eventually become Fs. Murray's therapist helps him establish small, specific goals rather than vague, long-range goals. The therapist also asks Murray to keep a diary of how he is spending his time when he is avoiding his studies. The method used to help Murray deal with his problem is _____ therapy.
    a. psychodynamic
    b. behavioral
    c. Gestalt
    d. existential

25. The social-learning perspective is to the psychodynamic perspective as _____ are to _____.
    a. bodily events; social and cultural forces
    b. social and cultural forces; bodily events
    c. environmental conditions; unconscious dynamics
    d. unconscious dynamics; environmental conditions

26. The process of saying freely whatever comes to mind in connection with dreams, memories, fantasies, or conflicts, in the course of a psychodynamic therapy session, is referred to as _____.
    a. systematic desensitization
    b. flooding
    c. free association
    d. exposure treatment

27. Which of the following is not a behavioral therapy?
    a. Flooding
    b. Skills training
    c. Exposure
    d. Unconditional positive regard

28. The primary goal of _____ therapy is to find meaning in life.
    a. rational-emotive
    b. reality
    c. existential
    d. transactional analysis

29. Which of the following pairings of problem and the most successful therapy for that problem is INCORRECT?
    a. Childhood behavior problems and existential therapy
    b. Specific phobias and systematic desensitization
    c. Depression and rational-emotive therapy
    d. Panic disorder and behavior therapy

30. The bond of confidence and mutual understanding established between therapist and client is called the _____.
    a. therapeutic window
    b. therapeutic alliance
    c. clubhouse model
    d. window of opportunity

31. An apparent treatment success that is due to the patient's expectation or hopes rather than the treatment itself is called _____.
    a. the placebo effect
    b. the nocebo effect
    c. the therapeutic window
    d. an empirically validated treatment

32. In _____ therapy, the therapist uses logical arguments to challenge a client's unrealistic beliefs or expectations.
    a. client-centered
    b. rational-emotive behavior
    c. existential
    d. aversive conditioning

33. Systematic desensitization and "flooding" are _____ therapies.
    a. behavioral
    b. psychodynamic
    c. reality
    d. Adlerian

34. Which of the following types of psychotherapists would be most likely to use free association and transference?
    a. Rational-emotive behavior therapists
    b. Behavior therapists
    c. Psychodynamic therapists
    d. Client-centered therapists

35. _____ is a humanist approach that emphasizes the tragic aspects of life, the burden of responsibility, and the need to face the inevitability of death.
    a. Social interest
    b. Psychoanalysis
    c. Existentialism
    d. Self-actualization

36. According to Carl Rogers, _____ is love and support given to another with no strings attached.
    a. the condition of worth
    b. unconditional positive regard
    c. existentialism
    d. self-actualization

37. Which of the following pairs of personality theorists and perspectives is INCORRECT?
    a. Abraham Maslow; existentialist
    b. Carl Rogers; humanist
    c. Carl Jung; genetic
    d. Sigmund Freud; psychodynamic

38. Which of the following terms is associated with transactional analysis?
    a. Free association
    b. Unconditional positive regard
    c. Irrational beliefs
    d. Complementary transactions

39. Which one of the following does NOT belong with the other three?
    a. Horney
    b. Glasser
    c. Adler
    d. Jung

40. The withdrawal of reinforcement until the conditioned response no longer occurs is known as:
    a. extinction
    b. elimination
    c. discrimination
    d. punishment

41. Freud is to ego, id, and superego as _____ is to parent, adult, and child.
    a. Jung
    b. Adler
    c. Perls
    d. Berne

42. Developed by Luft and Ingham, _____ asserts that there are four parts to the personality: the public self, the blind self, the private self, and the unknown self.
    a. neurolinguistic programming
    b. the concept of the collective unconscious
    c. the concept of the family constellation
    d. the concept of the Johari window

43. In which is the focus on the meaning of life and the relevance of the individual experience?
   a. Existential counseling
   b. Adlerian counseling
   c. Gestalt therapy
   d. Reality therapy

44. Popular techniques of this approach are role playing, "empty chair," and "making the rounds."
   a. Client-centered
   b. Psychoanalysis
   c. Gestalt
   d. Adlerian

45. Popular techniques of this approach are examination of client's memories, "spitting in the client's soup," and "catching oneself."
   a. Adlerian
   b. Psychoanalysis
   c. Rational-emotive therapy
   d. Reality therapy

46. In this therapeutic approach, the counselor's emphasis is on being authentic while concentrating on verbal and nonverbal messages.
   a. Existential counseling
   b. Behavioral counseling
   c. Gestalt therapy
   d. Rational-emotive therapy

47. Paradoxical intention, implosive therapy, and thought stopping are all techniques used by _____ counselors.
   a. Psychoanalytic
   b. Behavioral
   c. TA
   d. Reality therapy

48. Stress inoculation is a concept introduced by:
   a. John Krumboltz
   b. Joseph Wolpe
   c. Albert Bandura
   d. Donald Meichenbaum

49. According to Freud, _____ is the most important defense mechanism. An example of this defense mechanism is when a woman who has been physically abused by her spouse doesn't remember ever being hurt by him.
   a. regression
   b. repression
   c. reaction formation
   d. denial

50. A dog that has been trained to stop and stand at attention when she hears a duck call does not stop and stand at attention when she hears a goose call. This is an example of:
   a. stimulus generalization
   b. higher-order conditioning
   c. conditioned response
   d. stimulus discrimination

51. The disadvantage of closed-ended questions is that the client usually fails to:
   a. disclose personal information
   b. come up with an answer to the questions
   c. continue to dialogue with the counselor
   d. Both A and C.

52. Rational-emotive behavior therapy follows a five-step system using ABCDE, where D stands for:
   a. the affect
   b. the effect
   c. the external event
   d. disputing the irrational belief

53. The goals of this type of therapy include gaining knowledge about the self and recognizing and integrating the self.
   a. Adlerian
   b. Jungian
   c. Existential
   d. Freudian

54. In order to elicit a conditioned response, the neutral stimulus that will become the conditioned stimulus must _____ the unconditioned stimulus.
   a. follow
   b. precede
   c. occur at the same time as
   d. randomly occur sometime near

55. In contrast to feeling sorry for the client, the counselor needs to demonstrate _____ toward the client.
    a. empathy
    b. sympathy
    c. emotionality
    d. stability

56. In order to facilitate growth in a client, the counselor uses all of the following strategies EXCEPT:
    a. confrontation
    b. reflection
    c. abandonment
    d. interpretation

57. A(n) _____ schedule of reinforcement is the most difficult to extinguish.
    a. intermittent
    b. consistent
    c. systematic
    d. ratio

58. The primary distinction between reinforcement and punishment is that reinforcement _____ the likelihood of the behavior to occur again, while punishment _____ the likelihood of the behavior to occur again.
    a. increases; increases
    b. decreases; increases
    c. increases; decreases
    d. decreases; decreases

59. Negative reinforcement _____ the behavior by _____ a reinforcer; positive reinforcement _____ the behavior by _____ a reinforcer.
    a. increases, taking away; increases, adding
    b. increases, adding; increases, taking away
    c. decreases, adding; increases, adding
    d. decreases, taking away; increases, taking away

60. There are long silences, several members of the group are acting out, and it seems like all the group members are expressing frustrations with both the structure of the group and the way the group leader is functioning. Most likely this group is in the _____ state of the group process.
    a. working
    b. initial
    c. transition
    d. closing

61. From which perspective are the group goals to enable members to pay close attention to their here-and-now experiences so they can recognize and integrate disowned aspects of themselves?
    a. Gestalt
    b. Psychodynamic
    c. Reality
    d. Existential

62. Which of the following is NOT an advantage of group counseling?
    a. Cost-effectiveness
    b. Focus on individual needs
    c. Opportunities for feedback
    d. Structured practice

63. As a leader of a group, Barb is very structured. She sets and directs all of the group's goals and activities and hardly ever asks the participants for input. Most likely, Barb has a(n) _____ style of leadership.
    a. laissez-faire
    b. democratic
    c. authoritative
    d. authoritarian

64. What is likely to happen in a group when the leader is authoritarian?
    a. Members become dependent on the leader.
    b. Members become more motivated to achieve goals.
    c. Members lose focus on goals.
    d. Members have high morale.

65. All of the following are characteristics of an open group EXCEPT:
    a. Members can join and leave at any time.
    b. The number of sessions is undetermined.
    c. There is good cohesion.
    d. Group meetings are usually held in a hospital setting.

66. In contrast to a homogeneous group, a heterogeneous group:
    a. is more cohesive and supportive
    b. has members with greater awareness of themselves and others
    c. has less conflict among participants
    d. focuses on one specific problem

67. All of the following are assumptions of groups EXCEPT:
   a. The leader is a member of the group.
   b. Trust is a must.
   c. Much of the growth in groups occurs through observations, modeling, and social learning.
   d. There are often discrepancies among participants' expectations, hopes, and desires.

68. During the working stage of the group, the leader's role is to:
   a. establish a trusting climate
   b. provide a role model
   c. deal with feelings
   d. support risks

69. The emphasis for this type of group is on prevention and development of healthy behaviors.
   a. Secondary
   b. Tertiary
   c. Primary
   d. Homogeneous

70. There is a distinction between group content and group process. An example of group process would be:
   a. Sarah monopolizes the group by continuously talking and doesn't allow other participants to contribute to the discussion.
   b. Joe says, "I think today's topic should be what to do on a first date."
   c. Randy rolls his eyes every time Karen says something.
   d. both A and C.

71. Greg seems to make light of everything that goes on in the group. If someone is late, for example, he makes a humorous remark about calling for a search party. Greg would be described as the _____ of the group.
   a. joker
   b. dominator
   c. placater
   d. scapegoat

72. A counselor is conducting the initial screening of individuals who may be included in a bereavement group. An appropriate candidate for the group would be one who:
   a. has a severe mental illness
   b. lacks cognitive and thinking abilities
   c. is free from the use of alcohol or other drugs
   d. has a history of violence or uncontrolled anger

73. A group has co-leaders. That is, there are two trained counselors who are facilitating the group together. All of the following are advantages of co-leadership groups EXCEPT:
    a. More support and attention are provided to group participants.
    b. There is less time spent observing participants.
    c. Effective modeling of appropriate behavior is provided to the participants.
    d. Participants often view co-leaders as parents.

74. The group leader points out defenses, resistances, and transferences as they occur in this type of group.
    a. Client-centered group
    b. Psychoanalytic group
    c. Encounter group
    d. Transactional analysis group

75. Premature termination of participation in a group usually occurs when an individual is:
    a. not very motivated
    b. highly intelligent
    c. open to experiences
    d. empathetic

76. Career-oriented, successful ethnic minority women:
    a. face racial but not gender discrimination
    b. rarely receive support from other women
    c. tend to have mothers who had low expectations for them
    d. often display unusually high self-efficacy

77. The group that is most affected by the "glass ceiling phenomenon" consists of:
    a. women who are in careers most often populated by men
    b. men in middle management
    c. blue-collar workers
    d. stay-at-home mothers

78. Which group of students would be least likely to seek out career counseling?
    a. Students in high school or middle school
    b. None
    c. Students entering college
    d. Students who were taking college prep courses in high school

79. In dual-career families, the woman typically:
    a. starts her family before entering the workforce
    b. decides not to have children
    c. has an established career before having children
    d. None of the above

80. Compared with high school students who enter the workforce right after graduation, students who go to college can expect to:
    a. be hired at lower wages
    b. earn about $10,000 more per year
    c. work longer hours
    d. be hired to fill more unskilled positions

81. Leisure activities are those activities that a professional career counselor:
    a. may also refer to as avocations
    b. never discusses with clients
    c. describes as relaxing and done at work
    d. describes as involving going on vacations

82. Dual-career families engage in leisure time:
    a. more often than families with one wage earner
    b. that is more costly than that of families with one wage earner
    c. less often than families with one wage earner
    d. None of the above

83. The role of the professional career counselor involves all of the following EXCEPT:
    a. facilitating self-awareness
    b. teaching decision-making skills
    c. teaching employability skills
    d. None of the above

84. Career choices as expressions of one's personality are to _____ as career choices as influenced by genetic endowment, environmental factors, and previous learning experiences are to _____.
    a. Krumboltz; Holland
    b. Holland; Krumboltz
    c. Roe; Krumboltz
    d. Holland; Roe

85. One of the main premises of _____ theory is that individuals choose occupations that will permit them to use their competencies.
    a. Caplow's
    b. Super's
    c. Roe's
    d. Hoppock's

86. Super describes four stages of career development, beginning in adolescence with the _____ stage, in which a person fantasizes and role-plays in order to clarify the emerging self-concept. In the _____ stage the self-concept adjusts to fit the stabilized career choice and the person tries out various options.
   a. maintenance; establishment
   b. establishment; maintenance
   c. establishment; exploratory
   d. exploratory; establishment

87. All of the following are assumptions of John Holland's theory of career choice EXCEPT:
   a. Individuals can be categorized into six different personality types.
   b. People search for work environments in which their personality types can be expressed without much interference.
   c. Environment has very little to do with career choice.
   d. The behavior of an individual is determined by the interaction between the environment and the person's unique personality characteristics.

88. A career counselor who adheres to Holland's theory of career choice may have his clients take the _____ to help determine personality types.
   a. MMPI
   b. KOIS
   c. SDS
   d. SCII

89. Which of the following are postulates of Hoppock's theory?
   a. Everyone has basic needs, and a person's reaction to these needs influences occupational choice.
   b. People tend to move toward careers that serve their needs.
   c. Self-awareness and understanding are the bases upon which a person chooses an occupation.
   d. All of the above

90. Which pair seems to go together?
   a. Roe and Holland
   b. Holland and Krumboltz
   c. Roe and Hoppock
   d. Roe and Krumboltz

91. According to Roe, career choice is influenced by:
   a. genetics
   b. parent–child interactions
   c. unconscious motivators
   d. all of the above

92. Gender bias would be aroused by which of the following?
   a. A man who is studying to be a nurse
   b. A woman who is studying to be a nurse
   c. A woman who drives a semi truck
   d. Both A and C.

93. You are a career counselor who is interested in keeping up with trends in the job market so that you can better assist your clients. One of the best ways to keep up with the trends in the job market is to consult the:
   a. OOH
   b. DOT
   c. Wall Street Journal
   d. SOC

94. A 42-year-old woman returns to her career as an HR manager after her children start to attend school all day. This is an example of:
   a. a reentry woman
   b. a displaced homemaker
   c. gender bias
   d. wage discrimination

95. A receptionist at a dental office is not allowed to sing or hum at the office, but when she gets home, she turns on the radio and sings her favorite songs as loudly as she can. This is an example of:
   a. the contrast effect
   b. spillover
   c. the compensatory effect
   d. the recency effect

96. The 20th percentile represents:
   a. the score at or below which 80% of the scores in the distribution fall
   b. that the examinee correctly answered 80% of the questions on the test
   c. the score at or below which 20% of the scores in the distribution fall
   d. that the examinee correctly answered 20% of the questions on the test

97. A test is considered "standardized" if it includes:
   a. clearly specified procedures for administration
   b. clearly specified procedures for scoring
   c. normative data
   d. all of the above

98. Which of the following sources of information about tests would probably provide the best information about sources and trends in testing and assessment?
    a. Test critiques
    b. Journal articles
    c. Test manuals
    d. All of the above

99. Which of the following best describes norms?
    a. They give meaning to a behavior sample.
    b. They provide a parallel form for comparison.
    c. They indicate whether a test is reliable.
    d. They tell whether a distribution of scores is normally distributed.

100. Which of the following best describes a "good" test?
    a. It is reliable.
    b. It has norms.
    c. It is valid.
    d. All of the above

101. If college graduates typically earn more money than high school graduates, this would indicate that level of education and income are:
    a. causally related
    b. positively correlated
    c. negatively correlated
    d. unrelated

102. A researcher who observes a strong negative correlation between income and mental illness would conclude that:
    a. being poor causes mental illness
    b. having wealth makes one resistant to mental illness
    c. those with lower incomes tend to suffer from higher rates of mental illness and those with higher incomes tend to suffer from lower rates of mental illness
    d. lower income levels lead to lower levels of mental illness

103. A test producing the same results from one time to another is to a test measuring what it is supposed to as _____ is to _____.
    a. validity; reliability
    b. reliability; validity
    c. reliability; standardization
    d. standardization; reliability

104. Which of the following are measures of central tendency?
   a. Standard error of measurement and standard deviation
   b. Median and mode
   c. Range and variance
   d. Stanine and percentile

105. Which of the following pairs correctly describes forms of reliability?
   a. Equivalence and internal consistency
   b. Stability and concurrent
   c. Internal consistency and construct
   d. Concurrent and construct

106. Which of the following is TRUE of testing people with disabilities?
   a. Test scores administered under standardized and modified conditions are typically equivalent.
   b. General agreement exists on how tests should be modified for people with disabilities.
   c. There exists a need for a growing body of research related to the equivalency between tests administered under standardized and under modified conditions.
   d. Both B and C.

107. Which of the following is the best approach to minimizing or eliminating test bias?
   a. Creating separate norm groups for different groups against whom the test is thought to be biased
   b. Having a panel of experts review the test items before standardizing the test
   c. Pre-screening examiners to be used in the standardization process for any possible prejudicial feelings
   d. Screening test items for possible bias

108. Multiple-choice items like those found on the NCE tap skills primarily of:
   a. organization
   b. planning
   c. recognition
   d. recall

109. One method of calculating intelligence quotient (IQ) is:
   a. chronological age/mental age × 100
   b. chronological age/mental age + 100
   c. mental age/chronological age + 100
   d. mental age/chronological age × 100

110. Which of the following is NOT an intelligence test?
   a. WISC-IV
   b. WAIS-III
   c. MMPI-II
   d. WPPSI-III

111. MMPI-A and CPI are to _____ as Rorschach and TAT are to _____.
   a. interest inventories; subjective tests
   b. objective tests; interest inventories
   c. objective tests; standardized tests
   d. objective tests; subjective tests

112. The Rorschach, TAT, and Rotters Incomplete Sentences are all:
   a. projective tests
   b. observational tests
   c. rating scales
   d. standardized personality tests

113. One of the major criticisms of projective tests is that they:
   a. have too many questions
   b. are too subjective
   c. are too structured
   d. take too much time to administer

114. A counselor may decide to administer a number of personality tests in order to:
   a. better understand the client
   b. predict future performance
   c. evaluate the outcomes of counseling
   d. All of the above

115. The key difference between ipsative scales and normative scales is that ipsative scales:
   a. allow the counselor to make comparisons among individuals
   b. provide information about an individual client
   c. include achievement and aptitude tests
   d. have been standardized and normed

116. Jennifer, a Brandon High School graduating senior, took the Geneva Advanced Placement test in mathematics and earned 177 points out of a total of 200 points. This score means that Jennifer did as well or better than:
   a. 86% of the entering freshman at Coolridge Community College
   b. 73% of college students majoring in mathematics
   c. 89% of the graduating seniors at Glenbrook High School
   d. 77% of the mathematics team members from Highland High School

117. Terry's average score per basketball game is 27 points. This places him sixth among all the forwards in the Midwest basketball league. The level of measurement described in this example is:
    a. ordinal
    b. ratio
    c. interval
    d. nominal

118. A researcher reports a correlation coefficient of –.43 between the amount of television viewing by children and the number of times these children are on the honor roll at school. This means:
    a. Too much television viewing causes students' grades to be low.
    b. There is a moderately negative relationship between how much television a child watches and how often her or his grades are high enough to earn a position on the honor roll.
    c. There is very little relationship between how much television a child watches and how often her or his grades are high enough to earn a position on the honor roll.
    d. The more television a child watches, the more often the child's grades are high enough to earn a position on the honor roll.

119. A counselor wants to make sure that the test she is using provides the same scores for people when they retake the test a month later. What should the counselor look for when reviewing the test manual?
    a. Alternate or parallel-forms reliability
    b. Split-half reliability
    c. Scorer reliability
    d. Test-retest reliability

120. When applying to graduate school, the admissions committee compares the candidate's scores on the GRE with the candidate's grade point average reported on the college transcripts. This is an example of:
    a. construct validity
    b. content validity
    c. criterion-related validity
    d. concurrent validity

121. Only _____ permits a researcher to identify cause and effect.
    a. a correlational study
    b. an experiment
    c. a survey
    d. naturalistic observation

122. A hypothesis is:
   a. a defense mechanism
   b. a testable prediction
   c. a conclusion based on data
   d. none of the above

123. An experiment in which neither the subjects nor the individuals running the study know which subjects are in the control group and which are in the experimental group until after the results are tallied is called a _____ study.
   a. single-blind
   b. placebo
   c. double-blind
   d. confounded

124. A researcher wants to conduct a study looking at the effects of systematic desensitization on agoraphobia. In this case, the independent variable is _____ and the dependent variable is _____.
   a. agoraphobia; systematic desensitization
   b. systematic desensitization; agoraphobia
   c. systematic desensitization; group effects
   d. None of the above

125. A researcher reports that $p < .05$ in his study. This means:
   a. There is a less than 5% probability that the results obtained are in error.
   b. There is a greater than 95% chance that the results obtained are accurate.
   c. There is a less than 5% probability that the results are accurate.
   d. There is a greater than 95% chance that the results obtained are in error.

126. Of the following, which is the loosest acceptable p-value bound if a researcher needs to demonstrate that something is 98% statistically significant?
   a. $p < 0.05$
   b. $p < 0.01$
   c. $p < 0.001$
   d. $p < 0.10$

127. A Type I error is to _____ as a Type II error is to _____.
   a. accepting the null hypothesis when it is false; rejecting the null hypothesis when it is true.
   b. accepting the null hypothesis when it is true; rejecting the null hypothesis when it is true.
   c. rejecting the null hypothesis when it is true; accepting the null hypothesis when it is true.
   d. rejecting the null hypothesis when it is true; accepting the null hypothesis when it is false.

128. One way to reduce Type I and Type II errors is to:
    a. increase sample size
    b. decrease sample size
    c. increase the level of significance
    d. decrease the level of significance

not cause and effect!

129. If a researcher who found a negative <u>correlation</u> between the amount of TV viewing done by children and academic performance were to graph her results, she would use a:
    a. normal bell curve
    b. positively skewed curve
    c. scatterplot
    d. negatively skewed curve

130. A t-score has a mean of _____ and a standard deviation of _____.
    a. 100; 15
    b. 10; 2
    c. 50; 15
    d. 50; 10

131. A person received a t-score of 40. This means:
    a. Her score fell one standard deviation below the mean.
    b. Her score is very low.
    c. There is an error because you can't get a t-score of 40.
    d. Her score is higher than average.

132. A confounded study is one in which:
    a. there is a wide range of scores
    b. there is a random sample
    c. there are undesirable variables as part of the experiment
    d. undesirable variables are eliminated

133. Behavior changing as a result of just being part of an experiment is to the _____ as believing that someone with an extensive vocabulary is better at communicating is to the _____.
    a. halo effect; Rosenthal effect
    b. Hawthorne effect; Rosenthal effect
    c. Hawthorne effect; halo effect
    d. placebo effect; Rosenthal effect

134. The best kind of random sampling technique that would include 10% Asian, 10% Hispanic, and 15% African American, as well as individuals from the majority ethnic group, would be a:
   a. mixed randomized sampling technique
   b. stratified sampling technique
   c. cluster sampling technique
   d. random chance sampling technique

135. In experimental research, the researcher states a null hypothesis. A null hypothesis states that:
   a. there will be differences found between the experimental and control groups
   b. the differences between the experimental and control groups are due to chance
   c. there will be no differences between the experimental and control groups
   d. Both B and C.

136. An independent variable is the one the experimenter _____, while the dependent variable is the one the experimenter _____.
   a. manipulates; looks at for outcomes
   b. looks at for outcomes; manipulates
   c. leaves unattended; changes
   d. changes; leaves unattended

137. A researcher looks at one subject across time and takes numerous measurements throughout the process. This is known as a(n) _____.
   a. AB design
   b. ABAB design
   c. time-series or continuous measurement design
   d. correlational design

138. A researcher conducts a study in which she looks at the effects of using Nicorette gum on smoking cessation. Most likely, her statistical analysis will include:
   a. Pearson's r
   b. a t-test
   c. an ANOVA
   d. a chi-square

139. Ethical dilemmas often center on issues related to:
   a. dual relationships
   b. confidentiality
   c. credentials of test administrators
   d. licensure

140. The difference between confidentiality and privileged communication is:
    a. "Privileged communication" is a legal term and confidentiality is an ethical concept.
    b. "Confidentiality" is a legal term and privileged communication is an ethical concept.
    c. Privileged communication is enforced only when a client asks something to be privileged.
    d. Confidentiality is enforced only when a client asks that something be kept confidential.

141. A malpractice claim can be lodged against a counselor when:
    a. the counselor was negligent
    b. the client suffered physical or psychological injury
    c. a professional relationship was established
    d. All of the above

142. A counselor wants to discuss the treatment of a particular client with the client's physician. Ethically, the counselor should:
    a. call the physician on the telephone
    b. send a letter of introduction to the physician
    c. have the client sign a release-of-information consent form prior to any contact with the physician
    d. have the client talk to her/his physician

143. You are the counselor who is taking the on-call services for the evening. An individual calls asking you if her boyfriend is seeing a counselor at your clinic. Your best course of action is to:
    a. get the phone number of the individual and call her back with the information
    b. not acknowledge anything
    c. suggest that she ask her boyfriend herself
    d. provide her with the information she is asking for

144. You are a counselor who will be seeing a 15-year-old girl who has problems with anxiety. At the initial session, you have her guardian complete the intake questionnaire and sign a permission form giving you permission to treat the girl. You also:
    a. get all the financial information so that the insurance company can be billed
    b. discuss the limits of confidentiality with both the guardian and the teenager
    c. have the adolescent sign the consent form as well
    d. All of the above

145. The Code of Ethics is:
    a. legal and binding
    b. a hard and fast set of rules
    c. a set of standards of best practice
    d. All of the above

146. Which describes a violation of the "scope of practice" ethical standard?
    a. A counselor suggests a set of positive affirmations to her client after the counselor has discussed positive affirmations at length in session.
    b. A counselor uses EMDR with a client who insisted on this method of treatment.
    c. A counselor confronts her client about the negative thought patterns in which the client is engaging on a regular basis.
    d. A counselor seeks consultation from a colleague on a difficult case.

147. Tarasoff vs. Board of Regents of the University of California was a landmark case which brought to light the:
    a. duty of the counselor to warn individuals or groups about the potential of imminent danger
    b. standard of practice of obtaining releases of information in order to share information with individuals or agencies
    c. rights a client has as an individual with disabilities
    d. potential harm an impaired professional may inflict on his clients

148. A client jokingly talks about killing himself during a counseling session. The counselor should assess:
    a. whether the client has a plan of suicide
    b. whether the client has the means to complete suicide
    c. whether the client has a morbid sense of humor
    d. Both A and B.

149. The APA is a national organization for psychologists. The _____ is a national organization for counselors.
    a. APGA
    b. NCE
    c. ACA
    d. NASP

150. A 52-year-old counselor comes to work inebriated at least twice a week. He would be described as:
    a. an alcoholic
    b. an impaired professional
    c. a burn-out
    d. a workaholic

151. In the case described in Question 150, your ethical obligation as a colleague is to:
    a. confront him about his drinking problem and his impaired functioning
    b. report him to the police
    c. do nothing
    d. cover up for him by seeing his clients as well as yours

152. A man comes to you with a sexual dysfunction. You have very little experience in treating sexual dysfunctions. According to the ethical code, you should:
   a. do extra study on the topic as you continue to work with this man
   b. refer him to someone who has experience and training in the area of sexual dysfunctions
   c. tell him to use some herbal supplement to improve his condition
   d. ignore this problem and treat the man for depression

153. An 18-year-old student wants to view his educational records. Your course of action is:
   a. Get parent permission before disclosing this information.
   b. Talk him out of it.
   c. Give him access to these records, as the Family Educational Rights and Privacy Act affords him this right as an adult student.
   d. Ignore his request.

154. Your uncle asks you to counsel his daughter who is suffering from depression. This is:
   a. ethical
   b. not an ethical issue at all
   c. fine, as long as you let your uncle know what is going on in treatment
   d. considered a dual relationship and is considered unethical

155. You saw a client for a year and then terminated the treatment, as all goals were met. Six months later you call this client and ask her for a date. This is:
   a. okay, since you terminated the counseling relationship six months ago
   b. okay, since all treatment goals were met and none of them had to do with intimacy
   c. unethical
   d. not unethical but unacceptable

156. You have written a book and an accompanying workbook on managing panic. You require each of your clients who is being seen for a panic disorder to purchase your materials. This is:
   a. ethical, since these are treatment materials
   b. not unethical but unacceptable
   c. financially feasible for your clients
   d. unethical

157. You have written an article that you want to submit to a professional journal. This article needs to be in:
   a. MLA format
   b. APA format
   c. either MLA or APA format
   d. none of the above

158. A client wants to enter into treatment with you but does not have insurance. He reports that he can afford to pay you only $25 per session. Your usual fee is $100. In this case, you would:
a. refuse to see him unless he can pay your usual fee
b. charge him your usual fee and have him make installment payments
c. consider his financial situation and negotiate a reduced fee if this is warranted
d. make a referral to someone else

159. You are starting an eating disorders group. Ethically, you should _____ all possible candidates to make sure they are suitable for the group.
a. screen
b. diagnose
c. allow a sample session for
d. None of the above

160. A counselor who works for a county agency also has a small private practice. She screens all clients at the county agency and refers those clients with the best insurance benefits to her private practice. This counselor is:
a. following standard procedure for many public agencies
b. acting unethically
c. engaging in a dual relationship
d. practicing beyond her scope of practice

161. Under the ethical principles of informed consent, a counselor must inform each client of:
a. the limits of confidentiality
b. her credentials
c. issues related to third-party billing and missed appointments
d. Both A and C

162. A counselor who has not finished his dissertation has business cards that say "Dr. Dennis Browning, Professional Counselor." He is:
a. acting professionally and ethically
b. advertising himself appropriately, since he gives himself the title of Professional Counselor.
c. acting unethically by misrepresenting himself as having a doctoral degree when in fact he does not
d. not really acting unethically, since he does say he is a professional counselor

163. A counselor who has a current caseload of 124 clients decides to close his practice and move to Florida. If the counselor is an ethical professional, he would:
a. notify all his clients in writing of his plans
b. make referrals to other professionals for all of his clients
c. safeguard all client records
d. All of the above

164. According the DSM-5 criteria, a client that has previously met the criteria for stimulant use disorder but now has not met the criteria for stimulant use in 10 months (except for craving) would be termed to be in _____ remission.
 a. Full
 b. Partial
 c. Early
 d. Sustained

165. A "V" code in the DSM is the:
 a. clinical syndrome
 b. focus of treatment that is not attributable to a specific mental condition
 c. code used when personality disorders are present
 d. global assessment of function

166. Which name is associated with mental health consultation?
 a. Caplan
 b. Satir
 c. Adler
 d. Holland

167. A female client who was successfully treated for an eating disorder tells other women about her success and recommends you as the expert in treating eating disorders. You treat eating disorders as part of your practice but would not consider yourself an expert. Ethically, you should:
 a. inform your client and anyone she has referred to you that you are not an expert in treating eating disorders
 b. post your client's success story on your website
 c. accept any referrals without any further explanations
 d. ask her for a testimonial

168. Cases of _____ lead to the most malpractice lawsuits for any mental health provider, including counselors and psychologists.
 a. dual relationships
 b. failure of duty to warn
 c. sexual misconduct
 d. breach of confidentiality

169. The Education Act for All Handicapped Children (PL 94-142) requires that:
 a. all children who are handicapped be seen by a counselor who specializes in disabilities
 b. a free and appropriate education be provided for all children with disabilities
 c. children with handicaps be placed in the most restrictive environment in the schools
 d. children with handicaps be sent to special schools or institutions

170. You receive a referral from a family physician who attends your church. As a thank you, ethically you should:
  a. pay her for the referral
  b. send her a thank you letter
  c. have the physician tell everyone in your church to seek your services if they need mental health counseling
  d. treat her to lunch on a monthly basis

171. The DSM system of diagnosis is based on:
  a. a model set up by insurance companies
  b. an educational model
  c. the medical model
  d. an integrated model of doctors and lawyers

172. Which of the following is FALSE regarding family therapy?
  a. Family therapists believe that people's problems develop in the context of their families.
  b. Family members usually are aware of how they influence one another.
  c. Each family member is seen as forming part of a larger, interacting system.
  d. When one family member changes, each of the others must change as well.

173. The resolution of conflicts and breaking out of destructive habits are the primary goals of:
  a. family therapy
  b. existential therapy
  c. psychodynamic therapy
  d. couples therapy

174. A 22-year old college student comes to you for counseling following a visit to a hospital emergency room where he was complaining of chest pain. The medical work-up was negative. During your session you learn that his father recently died of a heart attack (a few weeks ago) while he was away at school, and that he is now experiencing episodes of sudden-onset fear accompanied by symptoms such as a rapid heart rate, sweating, tremors, chest pain, and shortness of breath, and feelings that he is about to die. After a short time the symptoms subside. In recent days he has been sleeping outside the hospital, fearful that he may not otherwise arrive in time when the symptoms strike. Which is the most likely diagnosis?
  a. Generalized anxiety disorder
  b. Panic disorder
  c. Somatization disorder
  d. Post-traumatic stress disorder

175. Active symptoms of schizophrenia involve an _____ of normal thinking processes; passive symptoms involve the _____ of normal traits and abilities.
- a. exaggeration; exaggeration
- b. exaggeration; absence
- c. absence; exaggeration
- d. absence; absence

176. As with many other systems, families aim to remain stable and reach equilibrium. This is known as:
- a. egalitarianism
- b. homeostasis
- c. equivalency
- d. predictive stability

177. One of the goals of family therapy is to help facilitate adaptability. Adaptability from a family therapy perspective means:
- a. obtaining a balance between stability and change
- b. reaching consensus
- c. obtaining a state of enmeshment
- d. reaching the status quo

178. A family of four comes in to see you. As the session begins, the two children and the mother seem to gang up on the father and try to pull you into this. Most likely this family is:
- a. triangulated
- b. enmeshed
- c. out of balance
- d. adversarial

179. During the past several sessions, a heated discussion has occurred between the father and the mother. The gist of the argument stems from the mother's constant attention being focused on the daughter. This is an example of:
- a. negative attention seeking
- b. disequilibrium
- c. enmeshment
- d. triangulation

180. A child who throws food at the dinner table is removed from the dining area and told to sit on the stairs for five minutes. This discipline technique is known as:
- a. coercion
- b. the Premack principle
- c. shaping
- d. time-out

181. A behaviorist family counselor instructs the parents of a 12-year-old boy to tell their son that when he gets his homework done he can play his Xbox. This is an example of:
    a. positive reinforcement
    b. the Premack principle
    c. quid pro quo
    d. negative reinforcement

182. One of the differences between individual therapy and family therapy is that family therapists believe in:
    a. family members acting independently of each other
    b. problems as involving one person
    c. a circular model of causality
    d. a linear model of causality

183. Family systems theory is to _____ as structural family theory is to _____.
    a. Bowen; Satir
    b. Bowen; Minuchin
    c. Minuchin; Satir
    d. Minuchin; Bowen

184. A marriage and family counselor treating a 10-year-old daughter and her mother tells the daughter that if she loads the dishwasher on Mondays, Wednesdays, and Fridays, then she and her mother will go shopping at the mall on Saturday. The counselor then has the mother and the daughter sign a contract to that effect. This is an example of:
    a. the Premack principle
    b. negative reinforcement
    c. shaping through successive approximations
    d. quid pro quo

185. Satir is associated with:
    a. integrated family therapy
    b. conjoint family therapy
    c. family systems therapy
    d. strategic family therapy

186. All of the following are goals of Whitaker's symbolic family therapy EXCEPT:
    a. boundary setting
    b. developing family nationalism
    c. maximizing languaging
    d. separating and rejoining

187. Compared with other counselors, family counselors tend to be more:
   a. rigid and inflexible
   b. nondirective and unstructured
   c. interested in maintaining their distance
   d. active, flexible, and structured

188. Haley assumes that:
   a. the client's symptoms are serving a protective function
   b. the power hierarchy of the family is confused
   c. the real problem is the family communication pattern
   d. All of the above

189. A couple comes in to see a counselor who specializes in sex counseling. Before the counselor agrees to treat the couple for sex counseling, she refers the couple for:
   a. a physical examination and medical history consultation by a medical practitioner
   b. a clinical assessment and interview
   c. sensate focus exercises
   d. an exploration of the marital relationship

190. The main purpose of sensate focus exercises is to:
   a. have the couple focus on communication patterns
   b. eliminate performance anxiety related to sexual functioning
   c. teach deep breathing and relaxation
   d. allow the couple to experiment with sexual positions

191. When working with blended families, a marriage and family counselor educates family members about the new dynamics within the family structure. More specifically, the counselor discusses:
   a. how adults and children come into the blended family with expectations from their previous families
   b. how parent–child relationships rarely change
   c. how a blended family begins after many losses and changes
   d. both A and C.

192. As founder of many child development centers, _____ could be attributed with being one of the first family counselors.
   a. Satir
   b. Ackerman
   c. Adler
   d. Rogers

193. Adlerian family therapy involves all of the following EXCEPT:
   a. overcoming feelings of inferiority
   b. promoting social interest
   c. pinpointing irrational beliefs
   d. investigating goals of behavior

194. According to conjoint family therapy, it is important to look at patterns of communication and meta-communication. Meta-communication can be defined as those aspects of communication:
   a. involving how something is said, not what is said
   b. involving what is said
   c. that are hidden
   d. that are direct and open

195. In family therapy, the terms "enmeshed" and "disengaged" are most closely associated with:
   a. Adler
   b. Minuchin
   c. Ackerman
   d. Haley

196. A 10-year-old boy refuses to eat at the dinner table with the rest of the family and often stays home when the family goes to the zoo or a museum. According to Minuchin, this youngster is _____ the family.
   a. disengaged from
   b. enmeshed in
   c. the placater in
   d. triangulated in

197. The role of the therapist in strategic family therapy is to:
   a. find the myth that keeps a behavior going
   b. understand levels of communication
   c. focus on levels of organization
   d. All of the above

198. One of the more common techniques used by marriage and family therapists is reframing. Which of the following is an example of reframing?

    a. A counselor listens intently to the family's discussion of an event and points out what happened at point A, point B, and point C.

    b. A counselor has the members of a family each take turns talking about how they felt about a specific incident.

    c. A counselor suggests that a mother's constant questioning of the daughter regarding a recent party the daughter attended could be interpreted by the daughter as mistrust rather than love and concern.

    d. A counselor outlines exactly how individuals in the family are to argue by setting up fair-fighting rules.

199. One family structure that is on the rise in the United States is the:

    a. blended family

    b. multigenerational family

    c. single-parent family

    d. homosexual family

200. True variance or the coefficient of determination is obtained by:

    a. subtracting the correlation coefficient from 1.00

    b. adding the correlation coefficient to 1.00

    c. squaring the correlation coefficient

    d. none of the above

Answers and Explanations

1. B: "Scaffolding" is a term used by Vygotsky that explains what Susie's mother is doing. She is adjusting her level of support to Susie based on Susie's level of performance. The zone of proximal development involves a range of tasks that are too difficult for the child to do alone but possible to do with the help of adults or other, more-skilled children. "Assisted discovery" is another term used by Vygotsky to describe learning situations that a teacher sets up within a classroom so that children are guided into discovering learning. Learning by imitation is a type of learning that involves a child watching someone perform a task and later performing the task by herself.

2. C: In Erickson's theory of psychosocial development, individuals who fail to achieve the goal of the lower level of development will have problems attaining the developmental task at the next stage of development. In the example above, the individual failed to achieve identity, which occurs during adolescence. Therefore, in young adulthood, the individual will have problems attaining intimacy, which is the developmental task to be achieved at this level. For autonomy, the individual would have to have failed to attain basic trust; for initiative, the individual would have to have failed to attain autonomy; and for integrity, the individual would have to have failed to attain generativity.

3. D: The best way to remember Freud's psychosexual stages of development is to think about what key tasks individuals do throughout childhood. The first thing infants do is suck (oral). Next, babies begin toilet training (anal), then discover the difference between boys and girls (phallic). Next, children spend time growing physically and cognitively but are latent in the psychosexual realm (not focusing on anything sexual); finally, puberty sets in and they begin to think about sex again and are focused on their own genitals.

4. B: The authoritarian parenting style uses coercive techniques and psychological control to discipline children, whereas the authoritative parenting style emphasizes some control but allows for some independence. The uninvolved parenting style rarely uses any control and the parent seems to be indifferent to the child's level of independence. In the permissive parenting style, the parents are typically overindulgent with the child. They exert very little control and are lenient when it comes to granting independence to the child.

5. A: In Harry Harlow's experiments, he found that baby monkeys preferred physical comfort to hunger satisfaction. In other words, the baby monkeys wanted to be close to a soft terrycloth "mother" rather than a wire-mesh "mother," even though the latter presented food. Therefore, attachment involves more than hunger satisfaction. It involves having close contact with a "loving" caregiver.

6. D: If someone is thinking about suicide, asking that person about suicide will not plant the seed or push her into committing suicide. It is important that as a counselor, you ask clients about suicide so that they can get the help they need. It is necessary to assess suicidality whenever you suspect that someone is contemplating it or behaving in ways that may suggest that she is contemplating it. It is best practice to assess for suicidality at each session with your clients. Suicide knows no age boundaries. Females attempt suicide at a rate three times higher than males, but males are successful more often, usually because they use more lethal methods than females.

7. B: Integrity versus despair is one of the stages in Erickson's psychosocial developmental theory. Kohlberg postulated that in the first level, preconventional, individuals are concerned with consequences imposed upon them for wrongdoing. Thus, in the example, Cody wanted to avoid being punished by having his television privileges taken away. At the conventional level, an individual wants to conform to societal rules so that authority rules and order is maintained. At the postconventional level, individuals define morality in terms of universal values and altruism.

8. C: Piaget proposed that there are four stages of cognitive development. The first stage is the sensorimotor stage, whereby the infant or toddler recognizes that even though something is out of sight, it still exists. Piaget's second stage of cognitive development is the preoperational stage (early childhood years) in which children begin to recognize that something can be an object as well as a symbol (dual representation). The third stage of cognitive development according to Piaget is called the concrete operational stage, during which children 6 to 11 years old develop the capacity of both conservation (object permanence, or the understanding that physical characteristics of objects remain the same even if the appearance is different) and reversibility (the ability to think through a series of steps and then to reverse the process mentally).

9. A: When you think about attachment and bonding, think about John Bowlby (1907–1990). Adler is associated with birth order and family constellation, while Freud is associated with psychosexual development. Piaget is associated with cognitive development.

10. D: One of the clues in this example is Henry's age. Another clue is Henry's discussion about his life successes and regrets, not finding another mate, being successful in school, or contributing to society. Erikson's generativity stage involves middle-aged adults who are launching their children, dealing with an empty nest, and working toward retirement. His ego integrity stage involves older adults who review their lives, looking at successes and regrets.

11. C: Instrumental aggression occurs when a child wants a toy that another child has and he tries to get that toy by pushing or attacking the other child in some way. Hostile aggression occurs when a child intentionally hurts another child because he wants to hurt the other child. Physical aggression occurs more often in boys than in girls and is any form of harm or physical injury such as pushing, hitting, biting, or kicking. Relational aggression

more often occurs in girls and involves the use of social exclusion, malicious gossip, or peer manipulation in order to damage another person's peer relationships.

12. C: The chromosomal abnormality, Down syndrome, is the most common chromosomal disorder, occurring in 1 out of every 800 births. Individuals with Down syndrome suffer from intellectual disabilities, memory and speech problems, and slow motor development. They usually have some heart deformities, as well as being of short and stocky build. They have almond-shaped eyes, a flattened face, a protruding tongue, and an unusual crease running across the palm of the hand.

13. D: Actually, Asian children usually have lower self-esteem than their North American counterparts, while African American children have higher self-esteem than their Caucasian counterparts. Generally, boys have higher self-esteem than girls. An authoritative parenting style is generally more accepting and less critical of children's negative behavior: Parents tend to build their children's self-esteem because the focus is on building a sense of worth and independence.

14. B: There is very little evidence to support that homosexual couples are poor parents. When gays and lesbians become parents, they generally are just as effective and caring as are heterosexual couples who become parents. The proportion of children who are maladjusted is just about equal for homosexual and heterosexual parents. The research shows that being gay or lesbian does not make a person a bad parent.

15. C: It was the social context that determined the behaviors of both the guards and the prisoners. In the Stanford prison study, the setting was so realistic that the participants became guards and prisoners. Their personal identities were masked by the context of being in a prison as either a guard or a prisoner. Even the researcher, Dr. Zimbardo, who took on the role of the prison warden, had to be reminded by one of his own graduate students that this was a research study and not a prison.

16. A: You can consider this logically. If you could hear another person crying or in distress, you would want to stop what you were doing in order to get the person to stop crying. Although having conflicting information being given to you would probably get you to think twice about it, you would not discontinue what you were doing. You would be confused. Milgram's team found that having someone who looked like an "authority" figure had an influence, but the opposite was not found to lead to disobedience. Subjects continued "teaching" in the "authority" and "nonauthority" situations. The study also found that peers did not have as great an impact as might have been thought. The only factors that influenced the participants were "authority" and hearing the cries of the learner. Consider this research as a study about a person's obedience to authority.

17. A: The most noticeable finding in the Stanford Prison Study was that the individuals who played one role or another really took on their role. As prisoners, these individuals in a very short time began to display behaviors such as distress and panic, which emulated the behaviors a "real" prisoner displays. It did not matter how the guards treated them or acted

toward them, the fact that they became like "real" prisoners was the key finding. Individuals who played guards took on behaviors of "real" guards; and individuals who played prisoners took on behaviors of "real" prisoners.

18. A: The key word here is "distort." As you attempt to answer this question, you need to think about how stereotypes distort the truth in negative ways. The most reasonable answer is that stereotypes distort one's ideas about how one group is so different from another group. In reality, the differences between groups are not as extreme as stereotypes make them out to be. People of differing cultures are not so different from people from another culture. It has been found that people are people, and we are more alike than dissimilar.

19. B: The best way to look at this question is to look at the choices Jennifer is given and her interpretation of these choices. Since Jennifer doesn't like either of the choices, this would be an avoidance-avoidance conflict. It is simply picking between the lesser of two evils. In an approach-approach conflict, a person likes both choices and has to pick the best of the best. In an approach-avoidance conflict, an individual both likes and dislikes a choice.

20. C: From a multicultural perspective, an emic view considers that an individual's culture matters. On the other hand, an etic view considers that people are people no matter where they come from or what their cultural background is. You might think about this distinction as emic = culture matters, and etic = total world. The distinction between autoplastic and alloplastic is that the former believes in the efficacy of changes taking place within the individual, while the latter believes in making changes in the environment. Think about it this way: When you drive an automobile, you are the operator, you're in charge.

21. D: It is not necessary that a counselor refer a client from another culture to another counselor. What is important is that the counselor demonstrates sensitivity to the needs of that client and has some knowledge about other cultures. Another way to look at this is to consider how you would treat someone who has an allergy to dairy products. You wouldn't give the person with allergies milk or ice cream. Instead, you would find out what the person with allergies can have and make adjustments based on that. You treat the person with allergies with sensitivity and get as much information about those allergies as possible.

22. A: The answer is pretty straightforward when you consider the other choices. The most appropriate standard of care for a counselor who works with multicultural clients is to treat each client individually. Special concern must be taken to ensure that the counselor is cognizant of her/his own biases; that the counselor becomes familiar with other cultures; and that the counselor can adapt her/his strategies and approaches to what is most efficacious for a particular client.

23. B: This question could trip you up if you are not aware of the cultural differences regarding eye contact. It is expected in our Western culture that we maintain good eye

contact at all times. In the Eastern traditions, however, eye contact is averted in some situations. It is the counselor's job to know those subtle differences and respect them.

24. B: When techniques involve setting goals or keeping a diary, you can automatically think that the therapy is behavioral. Most other therapies do not involve keeping track of behaviors or setting specific goals. A psychodynamic approach would use techniques like free association; gestalt approach would use techniques like psychodrama or exaggeration; and the existential approach would use imagery or awareness activities.

25. C: Whenever psychoanalysis or psychodynamics is mentioned, you should automatically think of unconscious processes, as this is the hallmark of such an approach. Of course, the social-learning perspective deals with social aspects, but more intently it deals with environmental conditions. Bodily events or bodily functions would be more aligned with a biological approach of some sort. Remember that learning involves interacting with the environment.

26. C: One way you can think of free association is as speaking freely about whatever comes to mind. Free association is a technique used by psychoanalysts and psychodynamic therapists. The other three techniques are all used exclusively by behaviorists.

27. D: The only technique that is not behavioral is unconditional positive regard, which is client centered, or Rogerian. To help you think about this, imagine a Rogerian-oriented therapist reflecting back whatever a client says as a way to show empathy or unconditional regard. Behaviorists do not address feelings at all, so unconditional positive regard would not be something a behaviorist would even consider offering to a client directly.

28. C: One way to think about the existential perspective is in terms of the human condition and what it means to be human; or in other words, what the meaning of life is. When it comes to rational-emotive therapy, think about the word "rational" and then attribute that to helping individuals move from irrational to rational thoughts. A good way to think about reality therapy is to focus on helping individuals formulate realistic plans for improvement. Transactional analysis involves looking at individuals' "transactions" as they go through their life scripts (parent, adult, child).

29. A: The clue here should be child behavior problems. Right away you should be able to eliminate existential therapy from that because behavior problems are best handled using behavioral techniques, not finding meaning. All of the other pairs are appropriate. When it comes to dealing with specific phobias, the treatment of choice is usually systematic desensitization, which is a behavioral technique. Depression usually involves having a client look at his/her own irrational thoughts that contribute to the depression. A panic disorder is also usually addressed using some sort of behavioral techniques.

30. B: The only realistic answer is the therapeutic alliance. The clubhouse model and window of opportunity have nothing to do with counseling. The therapeutic window

normally describes a range of time or doses of medication at which some positive effects will be noticed.

31. A: When improvement occurs just by the fact that someone is expecting improvement, that is the placebo effect. The opposite, the nocebo effect, occurs when an innocuous substance (a sugar pill) causes a person to get sick or to feel worse. The therapeutic window describes a range of time or doses of medication at which some positive effects will be noticed. An empirically validated treatment is one in which the treatment has been systematically tested and validated through some research and found to be successful.

32. B: In rational-emotive therapy, a client's irrational beliefs are challenged. In existential therapy, the focus is on the choices a client makes in order to find what is meaningful. Personal freedom and awareness are emphasized. In aversive conditioning, a person is conditioned using something aversive to stay away from or refrain from engaging in some inappropriate behavior. And client-centered therapy focuses on self acceptance and self exploration.

33. A: Behavioral techniques include: operant and classical conditioning, systematic desensitization, implosion, flooding, time-out, stress inoculation, and thought stopping. Techniques of the psychodynamic approach include: free association, dream analysis, and interpretation of transferences. Adlerian therapy techniques include: emphasizing client's strengths, examination of client's memories, focus on interpretation, and "spitting in the client's soup." Reality therapy techniques include: role playing, role modeling, defining limits, and helping the client make a plan.

34. C: The focus of psychodynamic therapy is bringing to the surface that which is unconscious; the therapist uses free association and transferences to make this occur. Another way to look at this is to remember that psychodynamic therapy has roots in Freudian theory. Freud spent much of his time discussing early childhood experiences and defense mechanisms. Think of rational-emotive behavior therapy as looking at irrational thoughts and beliefs. Strictly behavioral therapy looks at observable behavior, and client-centered therapy focuses on making clients feel good about themselves.

35. C: Think about existential therapy as looking at the human condition in its totality from birth to death and everything in-between. "Social interest" is a term synonymous with Adlerian counseling, while self-actualization is a term used by Maslow when he talked about his hierarchy of needs. Psychoanalysis looks at bringing what is unconscious to the conscious level.

36. B: If you remember one thing about client-centered counseling, unconditional positive regard is it. Carl Rogers emphasized personal warmth, empathy, acceptance, and genuineness when he described his approach. He focused on giving support and providing total acceptance without limits. You can eliminate conditions of worth because that is in direct opposition to what Rogers believed. Existentialism and self-actualization are not associated with Carl Rogers in any way.

37. C: Abraham Maslow is associated with existentialism and Carl Rogers is considered a humanist. When you think of Freud, you should automatically think of psychoanalysis or psychodynamics. Jung is a Neo-Freudian.

38. D: The key word here is "transactions." Transactional analysis looks at the interactions or transactions that occur within an individual (parent, adult, child). Free association is paired with the psychoanalytic or psychodynamic approach. Unconditional positive regard is affiliated with the client-centered counseling of Carl Rogers. And irrational beliefs are associated with rational-emotive behavior therapy.

39. B: Glasser is associated with reality therapy, while the other three are Neo-Freudians. Karen Horney is associated with object relations, Jung with the collective unconscious and archetypes, and Adler with birth order and family constellations.

40. A: All of the terms are associated with operant or classical conditioning except elimination. When Person A wants to eliminate a previously conditioned response in Person B, Person A withholds any reinforcement when the response occurs so that Person B no longer elicits the behavior. This is known as extinction. Discrimination occurs in classical and operant conditioning as well. Under this condition, a person learns to respond to only specific stimuli, while not responding to other similar stimuli. The person learns to distinguish between similar stimuli. "Punishment" is also a term associated with operant conditioning. It is a behavior modification technique that is used to decrease the probability that a particular behavior will occur again. Punishment can be either the presentation of an aversive stimulus or the taking away of a positive stimulus.

41. D: If you recognize "parent, adult, child," you would know that this set of terms is associated with transactional analysis, associated primarily with Eric Berne (1910–1970). Fritz Perls is associated with rational-emotive behavior therapy. Carl Jung is associated with analytic psychology, and Adler is associated with individual psychology.

42. D: Questions about the Johari window show up fairly often on this exam. It got its name from the two individuals who developed the concept—Joe Luft and Harry Ingham. They believed that clients come into counseling with all sorts of information, some of it known to the client and others, some unknown to the client but known by others, some known only by the client, and some unknown by everyone. Luft and Ingham believed that it is important to uncover that which is unknown. The collective unconscious is associated with Carl Jung. Neurolinguistic programming, or NLP, is a system of treatment that integrates psychology, linguistics, and communications. It was created by Richard Bandler and John Grinder. The family constellation is part of Adlerian counseling.

43. A: Any time you think about existentialism, you should think about philosophical questions such as, "What is the meaning of life?" and "Is there life in the hereafter?" The focus of Adlerian counseling is on developing and maintaining social interests. The focus of Gestalt therapy is congruence and the here and now. Reality therapy is focused on

becoming psychologically well by taking responsibility for oneself and formulating realistic plans.

44. C: It will be important for you to know some of the key strategies and techniques that the various therapies utilize. Gestalt therapy utilizes the empty-chair technique as well as psychodrama. Free association and dream analysis are popular techniques used by psychoanalysis. Adlerian counseling utilizes examination of clients' memories, catching oneself, and spitting in the client's soup. Client-centered counselors utilize active/passive listening, open-ended questions, positive regard, and reflection of feelings.

45. A: Adlerian counselors utilize examination of clients' memories, catching oneself, and spitting in the client's soup. Free association, analysis of transferences, and dream analysis are popular techniques used by psychoanalysis. Popular techniques used by reality therapy are role modeling, defining limits, and feedback. Counselors who use rational-emotive therapy often use homework assignments, bibliotherapy, and shame attacks.

46. C: In existential counseling, the role of the counselor is to be authentic and understanding of the client while stressing the personal relationship and sharing experiences. The role of the behavioral counselor is to assist the client in clarifying goals and modifying behaviors while teaching, directing, and advising. The rational-emotive therapist teaches, confronts, and corrects the client's irrational beliefs and ineffective self-talk. The role of the Gestalt therapist is to be in the present while helping the client resolve unfinished business and be congruent in verbal and nonverbal messages.

47. A: When you think about behavioral techniques, remember to include techniques employed in classical and operant conditioning (reinforcement, shaping, extinction) as well as systematic desensitization, implosion, flooding, time-out, and thought stopping. In psychoanalysis, the counselor relies on free association, dream analysis, analysis of transferences, and interpretation to advance therapy progress. A counselor who uses TA (transactional analysis) uses interrogation, confrontation, illustration, and concentration on early memories to assist clients. The reality therapist uses humor, confrontation, role modeling, role playing, and defining limits.

48. D: All four of these men are associated with behavioral counseling in some way, but Donald Meichenbaum developed the behavioral technique called stress inoculation training. The purpose is to help the client deal with future stress. The three-step process involves having the client monitor the impact of the inner dialogue on behavior when under stress, rehearsing new self-talk, and implementing new self-talk during the stressful situation. Joseph Wolpe developed systematic desensitization, which is a step-by-step process used to address phobias. John Krumboltz is more known in the field of career counseling but has written books on behavior modification. Albert Bandura is usually associated with social learning but more specifically with learning through observation.

49. B: Freud described some of the unconscious processes that individuals use to protect themselves from conflicts and anxiety. These unconscious processes are called defense

mechanisms, with the most important being repression. Repression occurs when a threatening memory, idea, or emotion is blocked from consciousness. Regression is a defense mechanism that occurs when a person reverts to a previous phase of psychological development. Denial occurs when a person refuses to admit that something unpleasant is happening. Finally, reaction formation occurs when an individual transforms his/her unconscious anxiety into its opposite outwardly.

50. D: Stimulus generalization occurs when, after conditioning, the subject responds almost identically to a stimulus that is similar to the conditioned stimulus. Higher-order conditioning is a procedure by which a neutral stimulus becomes a conditioned stimulus through the association with an already established conditioned stimulus. A conditioned response is a response that is elicited by a conditioned stimulus. It occurs after the conditioned stimulus is associated with an unconditioned stimulus. Stimulus discrimination occurs when a stimulus that resembles a conditioned stimulus fails to evoke the conditioned response.

51. D: If you think about this logically, you can see how A and C are correct answers. Closed-ended questions are those that can be answered with one- or two-word responses (e.g., yes or no). A client who is asked a closed-ended question answers the question or says yes or no and generally does not add any other information. When an open-ended question is asked, the client has to give more information in order to answer the question completely. The conversation continues and personal information is offered more freely.

52. D: The ABCDE system goes as follows: A is the external event; B is the belief about the event; C is the accompanying feeling; D is the disputing of the irrational belief that is causing the accompanying feeling; and E is the change that is made in the self-talk as a result of the therapy process.

53. B: Jungian therapists believe in a collective unconscious. Another key concept of Jungian therapy is the archetype. The goal of Jungian therapy is to transform the self by gaining knowledge about the self (collective unconscious, archetypes, personal unconscious) and then recognizing and integrating all aspects of the self (archetypes, etc.).

54. B: If you think about it logically, a neutral stimulus remains a neutral stimulus unless it can be associated with something that already elicits some sort of response. If a stimulus that already elicits a response is presented first, the response has already occurred. The neutral stimulus coming after the unconditioned stimulus (US) does nothing because the response has already occurred. Therefore, the neutral stimulus must be presented before the US so that it gets associated with the US and can then evoke a response similar to the unconditioned response. Although simultaneous occurrence with the US would evoke a conditioned response, in everyday life two things do not get presented at the exact same time very often. Presenting a neutral stimulus at random will not allow for any association to be made between it and the US.

55. A: A counselor needs to be able to understand the client's predicament, not feel sorry for the client. Understanding the client's predicament is called empathy. Feeling sorry for someone's predicament is sympathy and does nothing to empower the client. Although providing stability in the session, it is not what helps the client to work through the predicament. A counselor needs to keep his/her own emotions in check when working with a client. Emotionality on the part of the counselor usually serves to confuse the client or to add additional burden onto the client.

56. C: Confrontation is often used by counselors to point out discrepancies between a client's thoughts/beliefs and the behavior. Making the client aware of these discrepancies is a necessary skill for a counselor. When a counselor uses interpretation, she is pointing out the real meaning of a client's behavior. Reflection is another skill that a counselor uses to help clients. When a counselor reflects something back to a client, he is paraphrasing what the client said in order to emphasize the importance of the feelings associated with the statement and to project empathy. It is considered unethical to abandon a client.

57. A: If a person uses a slot machine, he gets some of his money back occasionally, but he still gets reinforced for using the slot machine. If you know that you will get money from a slot machine after every tenth try, the thrill is gone. It is still reinforcing, but boredom sets in. The unpredictability of an intermittent schedule of reinforcement makes it the hardest to extinguish because you don't know if you will get reinforced the next time or in five minutes or after twenty tries. All the other schedules of reinforcement are predictable.

58. C: All you need to remember here is that reinforcement increases the likelihood of a behavior occurring again, and punishment decreases the likelihood of the behavior occurring again. Reinforcements are positive and you want them, so you perform behaviors to get them. Punishments are negative and you do not want them, so you avoid performing certain behaviors so you don't get punished.

59. A: Don't confuse negative reinforcement with punishment. Negative reinforcement involves the taking away of something you don't like so that you get more of what you like. Positive reinforcement involves receiving something you like so that you get more of what you like. A child does his homework so that his mom will stop nagging him about doing it (increases by taking away a reinforcer). A child gets to watch a few extra minutes of a cartoon because he did his homework (increases by adding a reinforcer). The parent wants the child to do his homework.

60. C: There are five stages in the group process: forming, initial, transition, working, and closing. In the forming stage, the group leader recruits, screens, and orients potential group members. The initial stage involves tasks such as setting the ground rules, introducing members, and discussing confidentiality. During the working stage, members work on specific issues while sharing personal information. At the closing stage, the leader begins the termination process.

61. A: The goal of a psychodynamic-oriented group is to provide a climate to help members re-experience early family relationships. The goals of a reality-oriented group are to guide members toward learning realistic and responsible behavior and to develop identities that focus on success. The goals of an existential-oriented group are to provide conditions that maximize self-awareness and to remove obstacles to personal growth.

62. B: There are many advantages of group counseling, from cost-effectiveness to the ability to practice skills in a structured setting. There is a great deal of social support as well. Although members have their own individual needs and goals, the purpose of group counseling is for members to become better at interpersonal skills. Group counseling provides feedback and practice for all group members.

63. D: A laissez-faire leadership style could be considered a "hands-off" style in that there is no participation from the leader. The group participants make all the decisions and set their own goals and activities. A democratic leader encourages members to make their own decisions, and all members discuss the goals and activities. There is no authoritative leadership style as it applies to group counseling.

64. A: Typically, when there is an authoritarian leader, group members become very dependent on the leader. They usually are unmotivated and show greater hostility toward the leader. Their morale is usually low. In a group with a laissez-faire leader, the members continue aimlessly and lack direction. They have problems staying focused on their goals. On the other hand, a democratic leader inspires group participation, commitment, morale, and motivation.

65. C: Because group members can come and go at will, there is a chance that at each session there are different people. This characteristic of an open group lessens the cohesion of a group. At every session, someone new may join, and group participants have to get to know someone new. In order for a group to be cohesive, a greater amount of familiarity among group members is needed, as then they are more willing to open up and share with others. In an open group, it is also harder to nurture members and to sustain continuity compared with a closed group. A closed group has greater cohesiveness, stability, and predictability.

66. B: A heterogeneous group is usually more diverse than a homogeneous group. There may be a mixture of ages and genders. Another characteristic of heterogeneous groups is that there is a wide variety of problems as the focus of the group sessions. Homogeneous groups, on the other hand, are generally specific to gender and problem. The participants usually have common characteristics, which leads to strong bonds being formed among group members. Usually there is less conflict and greater attendance in homogeneous groups.

67. A: The leader is NOT a member of the group but is a trained expert. It is assumed that in a group counseling setting, trust is at the forefront. Without trust, no growth or exploration would take place. Trust also allows participants to share personal information with other

members of the group. Participants each enter the group with their own expectations, desires, needs, and hopes. These diverse expectations help members of the group discover things in themselves that would go unnoticed in other situations. Finally, growth occurs in groups through observations, identification with others, modeling, imitation, and other social skill learning processes.

68. D: The leader serves as a role model during the transition stage of the group, as well as establishing a trusting climate for the group, providing support, and addressing resistances and anxiety. During the termination stage, the leader's role is to deal with feelings, reinforce changes, and help members make plans. During the orientation stage, the leader's role is to help identify goals and structures and begin the modeling process. The leader in the working stage provides reinforcement, links themes, supports risks, and encourages translating insight into action.

69. C: There are three levels of groups—primary, secondary, and tertiary. Each level has a different focus or emphasis. The emphasis of a primary group is on preventing problems from occurring and developing healthy behaviors. The emphasis of a secondary group is preventative and remedial—its focus may be on the reduction of symptoms, lessening the severity of problems, and/or helping with overall adjustment to life stressors. The tertiary group can be thought of more as a "therapy" group in that its focus is on getting members of the group back to a more functional level of living. Tertiary groups may involve aspects of personality change and/or rehabilitation. One way to think about the three levels is in terms of severity—primary usually is very mild; secondary is mild to moderate; and tertiary is moderate to severe.

70. D: The distinction between group content and group process hinges on behavior. Group content involves the topics of discussion or the skills to be addressed. Group process involves looking beyond someone's words and instead observing the person's behavior. It's not what is said; it's how it is said. In the examples, Joe brought up a topic to be discussed (content). Randy reacted not so much to what Karen said, but rather to Karen herself. The act of rolling his eyes is a process (behavior pattern that he perpetuates). Sarah's constant monopolizing is her pattern of responding. It wasn't that she spoke often, it was that she dominated the discussion and didn't allow others to join in.

71. A: Group participants tend to take on different roles within the group, usually based upon how the individual interacts with others outside of the group. There are a number of different roles. Scapegoats generally take the blame for things that go wrong in the group. They allow others to point the finger at them without resistance. Placaters are the individuals in the group who try to appease everyone. They usually are uncomfortable with any conflict and are easily drawn to making concessions to keep peace in the group. Dominators or monopolizers are those who seem to control the group's discussions. They steer the discussion in the direction they want it to go. They seldom allow others to talk. Jokers, on the other hand, are those who make light of things, usually as a defense. They typically lack confidence and use humor as a way to detract or distract others from conflictual situations.

72. C: Individuals who have been diagnosed with severe mental illness, have histories of being violent or explosive, have limited cognitive or thinking abilities, are unable to communicate effectively, or use alcohol or other recreational drugs are not good candidates for inclusion in a group. It is important for all group members to feel safe, and having an individual who is prone to violence in the group may compromise safety. It is also important that all group members effectively communicate, process, and understand interpersonal relationships at a functional level. Therefore, individuals with limited capacities for any of these skills would not be good candidates for inclusion in a group. The process of a group is to learn and practice more appropriate social interaction skills. Someone who is incapable of understanding social interaction skills would not be a good candidate for the group.

73. B: Generally, co-leaders use a team approach. Each leader observes and processes what goes on in the group and provides feedback to participants. One leader usually cannot catch everything that goes on in a group. Leaders have to be aware of content, process, flow, and progress toward goals. Co-led groups give participants opportunities to observe how conflicts are handled between or among the leaders. The participants see the effectiveness of cooperation and harmony. Oftentimes, co-leaders are viewed as parental figures, and thus participants can learn more adaptive behaviors from well-functioning "parents."

74. B: In a client-centered group, the leader points out feelings, personal meanings, and individual attitudes. The function of this type of group is to increase self-understanding and altering of self-concepts. In a transactional analysis group, the leader focuses on life scripts and the dynamic ego states of parent, adult, and child and how these dynamic ego states impact others. In an encounter group, the leader focuses on the development of the individual, emotional experiences, and awareness of the behavior of others. A leader of a psychoanalytic group attempts to re-create, analyze, and interpret the participants' defenses, resistances, and transferences.

75. A: Research shows that individuals who prematurely leave a group are less intelligent, poorly motivated, and high in denial. They have difficulties trusting others. Individuals who continue through the course of group counseling are open to new experiences, trusting, willing to listen to others, and empathetic. Trust is the most important characteristic for individuals who participate in group counseling. If you think about it, if a person is trusting, he will be more willing to open up to others, share experiences, benefit from feedback, and empathize with others. People with more limited intelligence may not be able to maneuver social situations at an appropriate level of sophistication that is necessary for group success.

76. D: The only answer that makes any sense is an emphasis on self-efficacy. All of the other answers are false. If you think through this, you should have been able to choose the correct answer. If these women had mothers who had low expectations for them or did not receive much support from other women, then these women would not be successful. These women face both racial and gender discrimination.

77. A: The "glass ceiling phenomenon" refers to situations in which individuals are denied career advancement due to discrimination. This discrimination could be by gender, race, or physical infirmity, such as deafness. So in this question, answer B would be wrong because it refers to men. Stay-at-home mothers are not in the workforce, so they are not affected by this phenomenon, and blue-collar workers do not seek career advancement.

78. B: All students seek out career counseling or guidance of some sort, especially those in middle and high school.

79. C: Dual-career families generally are those in which both the man and the woman have some sort of professional career. They usually are established in their careers before they start a family. Generally, these couples marry later than those who go directly into the workforce after high school. The key vocabulary to look at here is "career," rather than "job." Having a career is generally more aligned with continuing education after high school.

80. B: This question is fairly easy to reason through. Individuals who go right into the workforce after high school graduation routinely earn substantially less than those individuals who go to college. Individuals who go to college would not be hired for unskilled positions, as they are overqualified. It would be hard to say whether or not the college-educated individuals would work longer hours than the non-college-educated individuals.

81. A: The professional career counselor refers to leisure activities as those activities or hobbies with which a person is involved outside of work. These activities are referred to as avocations. A career counselor would discuss these activities with clients in order to better understand them.

82. C: Suffice to say, dual-career families tend to have less free time due to work and family responsibilities. They may or may not be involved in expensive leisure activities which are similar to those of other families. Because no one is at home to take care of household duties during the day, these activities must be done after work, thus, dual-career families have less time to spend on leisure activities.

83. D: Career counselors are involved in all of these activities. They help clients become better aware of themselves, teach decision-making skills, and teach employability skills.

84. B: Krumboltz is a behaviorist and, therefore, is interested not only in genetic endowment but in environmental factors and learning experiences. Holland developed the SDS, which involves looking at an individual's personality characteristics and matching them to clusters of job skills or interests. Therefore, Holland believes that career choices are expressions of one's personality. Roe's theory is developmental and includes not only aspects of one's personality, but genetics, parent–child relationships, and one's early experiences.

85. B: Remember that Roe's theory has a developmental flavor to it, so her theory does not discuss personal competencies. Caplow's theory ascribes to birth order and genetics as strongly influencing career choices. Hoppock's theory defines career choice as being influenced by one's needs. Therefore, Super is the only answer that fits the question. His theory ascribes to the notion that one's self-concept is ultimately important in career choices. He believed that people choose a career based on their competencies—what they are good at.

86. D: If you reason based on ages, you may have been able to figure this one out. What do adolescents do? They explore career options, fantasize about various careers, and role-play as a means to narrow down their choices. Thus, they explore. In the establishment stage, individuals try out options and establish their careers. The maintenance stage is where the career path has already been established and now is being maintained.

87. C: John Holland based the SDS on the six different categories of personality types. He believed that individuals choose careers based on personality types and environmental influences. An individual's behavior is determined by the interaction between environment and personality.

88. C: You need to be familiar with these different assessments. The MMPI (Minnesota Multiphasic Personality Inventory) is usually used by clinical psychologists to clarify diagnoses of mental disorders. The KOIS is the Kuder Occupational Interest Survey, which looks at matching career choices with interests, not personality characteristics. The SDS (Self-Directed Search) is the instrument developed by John Holland that looks specifically at six different categories of personality characteristics that may relate to certain career choices. The SCII (Strong Interest Inventory) is similar to the KOIS, as it looks at matching personal interests with possible career choices.

89. D: Hoppock's theory of career choice suggests that people choose careers that meet some personal needs. As part of this theory, Hoppock postulates that everyone has personal needs and that an individual reacts to these needs when making career choices. Making career choices involves self-awareness and understanding.

90. C: Hoppock and Roe are classified as developmentalists when it comes to career choices. They believe that early development and early experiences have a large impact on career choice. Krumboltz is a behaviorist and does not ascribe to early development an influence on career choice. Holland believes that environment interacts with personality characteristics when one chooses a career. Krumboltz and Holland believe that the environment plays a role in career choice, but Krumboltz looks at learning, not personality.

91. D: Roe has a psychoanalytic perspective on career choice, so she believes that genetics, parent–child relationships, and unconscious motives interact. If you think about psychoanalytic theories in general, you would know that all of the aforementioned dynamics influence an individual.

92. D: Gender bias goes both ways. Men in female-dominated careers and women in male-dominated careers can experience discrimination. So, a man seeking to be a nurse (a female-dominated career) and a woman seeking to be a semi-trailer truck driver (a male-dominated career) might experience discrimination on the job.

93. A: Here again, you need to know what these are. The OOH is the Occupational Outlook Handbook. This handbook provides information about trends in occupations, as well as statistics about salaries and wages. The DOT is not the Department of Transportation; it is the Dictionary of Occupational Titles and is obsolete. It has been replaced by the Occupational Information Network (O*NET). Basically, the DOT listed nine occupational categories such as professional, technical, managerial, clerical, and sales careers. The Wall Street Journal is a reliable source for information about the financial and business world but is not a source for looking at trends in occupations. The SOC is the Standard Occupational Classification Manual, which classifies types of activities associated with different careers. It does not provide information about trends in occupations.

94. A: You might think that this example relates to a displaced homemaker, but the key word here is "returns." A displaced homemaker never worked outside of the home. A reentry woman is one who had worked, decided to be a stay-at-home mother until her children were old enough to be in school all day, and then returned to work in her chosen profession. Gender bias relates to experiencing discrimination for being in a job that is dominated by the opposite sex. Wage discrimination relates to earning less than someone else, yet doing the same job.

95. C: You can think of the compensatory effect as being a reaction to being restricted from doing something. You want to do the activity, but you can't, so when you can, you really do it up right. You compensate for it. In this example, the woman isn't allowed to hum or sing at the office, but when she is away from work, she hums and sings to her heart's content. The contrast effect involves two individuals being interviewed for the same position. One qualified candidate is viewed in a less favorable light after a very well qualified candidate is interviewed first. Spillover occurs when an individual engages in activities at home that are similar to those involved in his job. The recency effect takes place when a supervisor judges an employee's performance on the employee's most recent performance, with no consideration for performance at other times.

96. C: The best way to think about percentiles is to think of 100 people standing in a row. Each person represents one percentile from the 1st percentile to the 100th percentile. So in this case, the 20th percentile represents the twentieth person in the "distribution." So, it is the place where the twentieth person stands in the line. If the answer were A, then it would be the place in the line where the eightieth person would stand. In contrast, a percentage score is what is described by answer B or D. These two answers represent the percent of the questions the person got correct on a test. Most of us are familiar with percentages, as most teachers report percentages to you.

97. D: A standardized test must have standard procedures for administering, scoring, and interpreting the test. There must also be a set of norms to which a particular score is compared. Not all tests are standardized. For example, unless it is a test like the NCE or GRE, it is probably a test that was developed by a teacher or company. Tests may be administered the same way to everyone and scored the same, but if there are no norms to which to compare an examinee, it is not considered a standardized test.

98. D: If you want to investigate a particular test, best practice would be to read test critiques in books like Tests in Print or Buros Mental Measurements, read journal articles about that particular test, and test manuals. You wouldn't base a big decision on one source of information, nor would you do that when investigating a test.

99. A: The main purpose of norms is to provide meaning to test scores. A score of 100 means nothing if you don't know what receiving a score of 100 means. Is it an IQ score, where 100 is exactly average? Is it the score on the NCE (a failing score)? Is it a bowling score? Norms provide a basis for comparison of scores against each other and against the standard. If you know the standard, you can make comparisons. Answer B and C refer to concepts in reliability. Knowing if a distribution is normal gives the test user information, but knowing that a distribution is normal does not give you information about the norms themselves.

100. D: When you are looking for a test, you want the best available test for your purposes. A good test is valid and reliable and has a set of norms. Most important among these is validity. Remember, validity refers to a test measuring what it purports to measure.

101. B: When correlations are discussed, the key thing to remember is that you cannot say anything about one variable causing the other. You can only refer to one variable being related in some way to the other variable. In the case presented, the more education a person has, the higher the person's salary will be. This describes a positive correlation in that as one variable increases, the other variable also increases. A negative correlation would be: The hotter the temperature outside, the less hot soup people consume. In a negative correlation, one variable increases while the other variable decreases.

102. C: Here again, when talking about correlation; you cannot describe any causality. A, B, and D describe causation in some form. Look for key words to know if something is causal (causes, leads to, makes you, etc.).

103. B: By definition, reliability refers to how consistent over time a test is. Validity is defined as having a test measure what it is supposed to measure. Standardization refers to a set of procedures that are consistently followed for each administration of a test. Although it describes consistency, it is not related to the test itself. Standardization refers to the procedures implemented while giving a test.

104. B: Measures of central tendency refer to the mean, median, and mode of any distribution. It describes "average" scores. If you think about the bell curve, the measures of

central tendency are those that are in the middle of the distribution. Stanines and percentiles are types of scores, and range and variance are actually related to measure of variability, not central tendency.

105. A: Reliability involves consistency and equivalence. When a test is reliable, it is means that a test taker would receive nearly the same score every time the test taker would take the test. Another form of reliability is equivalence. A person who takes one form of a test would be expected to have nearly identical scores on another form of that test. Terms such as "concurrent" and "construct" refer to types of validity. "Stability" would be a term relating to reliability.

106. C: Tests administered using modified conditions may or may not yield results equivalent to those obtained using standardized conditions. There are no general agreements about how to modify tests for individuals with disabilities. Since testing individuals with disabilities is a fairly new concept, more research is needed to investigate equivalency of modified test administrations to standardized test administrations. Another topic of further consideration is how the test examiner will interpret results when a test has been modified.

107. A: Test bias refers to anything within a test that is unfair to an individual or group, such as asking questions about Wisconsin to people who live in Australia and who have never been in Wisconsin. In this example, the test developer could minimize test bias by developing norms for Australians who take the test and using those norms when an Australian takes the Wisconsin test. Answers B, C, and D may be only minimally helpful in eliminating or minimizing bias in testing.

108. C: Multiple-choice questions of any sort tap into a person's recognition memory. The person is given information from which to choose the correct answer. Recall is tapped using short-answer essays or a fill-in-the-blank format. Test takers are provided with very little information and must rely on their own recall memory to retrieve the answers. Organization and planning have no relevance here.

109. D: You can eliminate the addition of 100 because a ratio such as that derived from the first part of the formula added to 100 would yield a score around 100 with some part of a fraction. Here's how you can reason out the correct answer. Suppose a person is 10 years old exactly and earns a mental age of 10 years exactly; the person's IQ would be 100 because the fraction of 10 over 10 is 1, which multiplied by 100 is 100. If this same 10-year-old earns a mental age of 5, then multiplying the 10 over 5 (2) by 100 would yield an IQ of 200 (not possible). So, reversing the formula, a mental age of 5 for a 10-year-old (MA/CA) would yield an IQ of 50 (more reasonable considering the data provided). So, having a high mental age over any chronological age would yield a high IQ. Conversely, having a low mental age over any chronological age would yield a low IQ.

110. C: The MMPI-II is a personality test (the Minnesota Multiphasic Personality Inventory, second edition), while all of the others are part of the Wechsler series of intelligence tests.

The WISC-IV is the Wechsler Intelligence Scale for Children–fourth edition and is for children aged 6 to 16. The WAIS-III is the Wechsler Adult Intelligence Scale–third edition and is for adults. The WPPSI-III is the Wechsler Preschool and Primary Scales of Intelligence–third edition and is for children between the ages of 3 and 7 years, 3 months.

111. D: The differences we are looking at here are the differences in the formats of tests. The MMPI-A (Minnesota Multiphasic Personality Inventory–Adolescent) and CPI (California Personality Inventory) are based on a true/false format with a fixed choice. They are paper and pencil objective tests, while the Rorschach and TAT (Thematic Apperception Test) are projective tests that are subjective in nature. The answers to the stimuli are unlimited. There are no fixed choices. The test taker makes up answers based on the stimulus being presented.

112. A: The Rorschach is an inkblot test. The TAT (Thematic Apperception Test) is a storytelling test. The Rotters Incomplete Sentences test is a finish-the-sentence test. All of these tests are projective tests because they ask test takers to project their own thoughts and ideas into the stimuli to complete the answers. The test takers come up with their own answers freely without any suggestions or information being provided by the examiner except the stimuli. Rating scales are typically used to describe various dimensions of behavior across a number of different situations or environments. Standardized personality tests include the MMPI-II and CPI, among others. Observational tests would typically involve the examiner observing the test takers' behavior across environments or situations.

113. B: Projective tests usually do not involve any "questions" per se. Remember, the test takers come up with their own answers based on the stimuli presented. Projective tests by their very nature are not structured at all. Usually the instructions the examiner gives are minimal, e.g., "What might this be?" for the Rorschach. Projective tests do take a great deal of time, but this is not the major criticism. Projective tests are very subjective, and the scoring is also very subjective, despite there being scoring manuals for these tests.

114. D: If a counselor decides to administer a psychological test, most likely the counselor wants to understand the client more fully. The counselor may want to predict the future performance of a client. Or the counselor may want to evaluate the outcomes of treatment. A psychological test provides a means to look at these issues objectively and concretely.

115. B: An ipsative scale gives information about a single individual. There are no comparisons made between the individual and others. A normative scale gives information about individuals but allows the examiner to make comparisons between the single individual and others. So the key difference between ipsative scales and normative scales is whether comparisons can be made. No comparisons can be made when an ipsative scale is used.

116. C: Although Jennifer's score (177 out of 200) remains the same, the interpretation of her score will be different based on the norm group to which her score is being compared.

It is inappropriate to compare Jennifer (a graduating high school senior) to entering freshmen at a community college, to a group of college mathematics majors, or even to a group of high school mathematics team members, because Jennifer is not a member of any of these groups. She is a graduating senior from high school. Therefore, it is most appropriate to compare Jennifer's score to a similar group of graduating seniors'. It is important to compare one's score to a norm group closest to the group to which the individual belongs.

117. A: There are four levels of measurement. The most basic level is the nominal scale. There are no numerical values assigned, but nominal data fit into categories such as gender, numbers on a basketball jersey, or country of origin. Ordinal scale data involve rankings or order of people or objects based on a particular attribute. The numbers assigned for an ordinal scale have meaning only within the particular group. Interval scale data are calculated with the assumption that each number represents a point that is an equal distance from the point adjacent to it. Temperature is an example of an interval scale datum. Ratio scale data have an absolute zero. Weight is an example of a ratio scale datum.

118. B: When a correlation coefficient is presented, there cannot be an inference that one behavior or action predicts or causes the other behavior or action. There is no cause and effect when a correlation coefficient is presented. Correlation coefficients range between –1.0 and +1.0. The closer the coefficient is to 1, the stronger the relationship. If the coefficient is negative, this suggests that as one behavior increases, the other behavior will decrease. In the example above, the more television a child watched, the lower a child's grades were. A strong relationship is usually ±0.55 or above, while a moderate relationship is usually in the ±0.54 to ±0.30 range. No relationship is indicated by a correlation coefficient of 0.0.

119. D: Alternate or parallel forms of reliability involve giving two different versions of the same test to the same group of people. If the test is reliable, there will be very little difference between the scores received on both tests. Split-half reliability involves dividing a test into two parts and comparing the scores on the first part with the scores on the second part. If the test is internally consistent, the scores on each half of the test will be nearly identical. Scorer reliability is used when two or more individuals score the same test. If the test has scorer reliability, each scorer scores nearly all the items on the test the same way. Test-retest reliability involves obtaining nearly identical scores on the same test even when the test is given at a later date.

120. C: Construct validity is described as the extent to which a test measures a specific theoretical construct, such as the construct of self-esteem. Content validity is described as the extent to which the items on a test are examples of the construct that the test measures. Criterion-related validity is described as the extent to which a test correlates with independent behaviors or events. In the case of this question, the independent behavior or event is the student's grade point average used as a measure of academic success. Concurrent validity is described as a form of criterion-related validity whereby the test

administration and criterion measure happen at almost the same time. This method of criterion-related validity is not predictive.

121. B: Cause and effect is attainable only through an experiment. A correlational study looks only at the relationship between variables. A naturalistic observation involves simply observing subjects in their own environment. No cause and effect is even intended here. A survey involves distributing a questionnaire or survey to participants. Again, no cause and effect is intended.

122. B: "Defense mechanism" is a term used in psychodynamic theory that refers to the unconscious distortions of reality that people make. A hypothesis is a hunch or assumption that a researcher starts with when designing a study. The researcher wants to verify whether or not this hunch or assumption is true. It is what the researcher is testing. It is not the conclusions that the researcher makes based on the data obtained.

123. C: A single-blind study is one in which only one part of the team is unaware of who is receiving the treatment. In a single-blind study, either the researcher is unaware or the participants are unaware; not both. The way to remember this is that single means one and double means two. The team consists of the researcher and the participants. So, you need to look at whether only one part of the team is unaware or both parts of the team are unaware. A placebo effect has occurred when a participant reports improvement where the treatment was really nothing more than water or a sugar pill. In a confounded study, variables that are not wanted in the study come into play.

124. B: The best way to remember the difference between the independent and dependent variable is to look at the wording. If the question starts out with "the effects of," that is going to be the independent variable. The independent variable is the one that the researcher is going to manipulate. The dependent variable is going to have the word "on" close to it. In the question, the researcher wanted to look at the effects of systematic desensitization on agoraphobia.

125. B: This can be tricky. With a p < .05, if the researcher were to replicate his experiment 100 times he would get the same results at least 95% of the time. This means that there is a greater than 95% chance that the results found in the experiment are accurate. Basically, a p value <.05 rules out errors in the study.

126. B: A 98% chance of statistical significance equates to a p-value of <0.02. Of the choices listed, B and C are both less than 0.02, but the question asks for the loosest bound, so the correct answer is 0.01.

127. D: In a Type I error (or alpha error), the researcher rejects the null hypothesis when the null hypothesis is actually true (there are no differences between groups). In a Type II error (beta error), the researcher accepts the null hypothesis when the null hypothesis is actually false (there are differences between groups).

128. A: The best way to reduce errors in research is to have a large sample size—the larger the better. If you reason this out, you can see why. If you have 10 participants and 8 of the participants improved, you would say that is pretty good. If you have 100 participants and 80 of them improve, you would also say that is pretty good. Both of these situations leave some doubt, however. If you have 1000 participants and 800 improve, you would feel much better about stating that 800 participants improved.

129. C: When you think of a correlational study, you should automatically think of a graph with a bunch of dots on it. There is an x-axis and a y-axis and a bunch of dots. The researcher tries to find a line of best fit by visualizing where variable X is in relation to variable Y. Notice, I said "in relation to." In a correlational study, the researcher is looking for the relationship between variables, not cause and effect. A positively or negatively skewed curve and a normal bell curve are usually associated with cause and effect.

130. D: You will have to know the means and standard deviations of the various statistics used in research. Do not confuse a t-score with an IQ score. An IQ score has a mean of 100 and a standard deviation of 15. A z-score expresses the number of standard deviations that a raw score is from the mean. A t-score has a mean of 50 and a standard deviation of 10.

131. A: Remember that a t-score has a mean of 50 and a standard deviation of 10. In this situation, the test taker received a t-score of 40. That score is one standard deviation below the mean. It is neither a very high nor a very low score. You might consider t-scores of 70 and 30 to be high and low, respectively. A t-score of 70 is two standard deviations above the mean, while a t-score of 30 is two standard deviations below the mean.

132. C: If something is confounded, it is confusing or befuddling. Therefore, when looking at research, if you cannot distinguish between variables or if things are not clear, then a study is confounded. Usually that means that there are variables that the researcher did not control or eliminate.

133. C: The halo effect is the tendency to generalize about a person based on one trait. In the question, the researcher believed that a person with a very good vocabulary would be a good communicator. He based his belief on one trait—having a good vocabulary. The placebo effect is when an ineffective or inert substance is given to participants and participants report positive changes. Because the substance is inert or ineffective, there actually should not be any changes. The Rosenthal effect or Pygmalion effect suggests that the researcher's beliefs impact the outcome of an experiment. In contrast to the halo effect, the Rosenthal effect is more a component of the researcher's beliefs, not the participant's traits themselves. The Hawthorne effect is the tendency for participants to change their behavior just because they are participants in a research study.

134. B: There really is no mixed randomized sampling technique. A cluster sampling technique involves taking a smaller sample from a larger sample. In cluster sampling, the groups are randomized, not the individuals in the groups. A random chance sampling technique involves the simple randomness involved in choosing people at random

regardless of any characteristics or group identities. Each person has an equal chance of being chosen. In a stratified sampling technique, different subpopulations are included in the random sample based on percentages of the subpopulations in the larger population. For example, if a researcher wants a representative sample from the general population, she would want an equal representation of males and females. Therefore, she would randomly choose half of her sample from the male subpopulation and half from the female subpopulation.

135. C: A null hypothesis is one in which the researcher states prior to beginning the research that there will be no differences between groups and that the differences found will be due to chance and not due to being in one group or another. The research hypothesis states that there will be differences between the experimental and control groups and that the differences are due to something other than chance (i.e., the manipulation of the independent variable).

136. A: The independent variable is the one that the researcher manipulates or changes. The dependent variable is "dependent" upon the changes that the researcher is making. So the dependent variable is the one that shows whether or not the manipulation of the independent variable is effective. The dependent variable is related to outcomes. Leaving variables unattended is not appropriate in most experimental research.

137. C: A correlational research design looks at the relationship between two variables (the amount of TV viewing and academic performance). An AB or ABAB design is a two-part continuous measurement design in which the experimenter has established a baseline (A) and introduces an intervention (B). The ABAB design is intended to rule out confounding variables by seeing whether the second AB pattern yields the same results. A time-series or continuous measurement design looks at one person across time using a number of measurements throughout the study. An AB or ABAB design is not performed across a series of time elements.

138. B: Pearson's r is used in correlational studies. An ANOVA is used when there is more than one independent variable or more than one experimental group. A t-test is performed when there is one independent variable, one experimental group, and one control group. A chi-square is used to determine if obtained results differ at all from chance.

139. B: The key word here is "often." Yes, ethical dilemmas related to dual relationships do come up, but in terms of volume or frequency, confidentiality issues come up more often those involving dual relationships, credentials of test administrators, or licensure.

140. A: Although the two terms may seem to come up within similar contexts, "privileged communication" is a legal term and "confidentiality" is an ethical concept. Things said during sessions are kept confidential within limits. Legally, when a counselor invokes privileged communication, this means that things revealed in confidential therapy sessions cannot be disclosed in court without the client's permission. The only exceptions would be when a mental health professional who has been hired by the court conducts an evaluation

or other service that relates to some legal action. In these cases, the counselor or other mental health practitioner has to inform the client of the limits of privileged communication.

141. D: If you think about this question, you can see that malpractice claims almost exclusively deal with a counselor's behavior that ends up harming the client in some way. Negligence on the part of the counselor could lead to potential harm to the client. Of course, any physical or psychological injury to a client harms the client. You may have stumbled on this question because of response C. If there never was a professional relationship established, then the counselor cannot be sued for malpractice. A professional relationship is established usually within the first few sessions and involves informed consent, discussion of the limits of confidentiality, and the process of therapy. If these components were not established early on in the relationship, then there really is no professional relationship.

142. C: A counselor who wants to consult or contact another professional, a client's family member, or someone else who works with a particular client must have the client give written permission to contact and share information. If the counselor gets contacted by someone who has contact with the client, the counselor cannot even acknowledge that the client is being seen unless the client has signed a release-of-information.

143. B: Similar to Question 4, the counselor cannot even acknowledge that the client is being seen by someone at the clinic. Be prepared with a uniform statement that all counselors at your clinic use in situations like this.

144. D: Just like you would do with any new client, you would have the parent or guardian provide some background information and get insurance information. Each state has guidelines about when adolescents must sign their own consent-for-treatment forms, but usually the age is 14 or 15.

145. C: A code of ethics is not a legal and binding document, nor is it a set of strict rules by which counselors must abide. It is really a guideline or a set of standards for best professional and moral conduct. There usually are no right or wrong answers to ethical dilemmas. When you run into an ethical dilemma, discuss it with other counselors and/or contact your profession's ethics committee.

146. B: EMDR (eye movement desensitization and reprocessing) is a specialization that requires additional training. Unless the counselor took the specialized training and had supervision, she cannot use EMDR in her practice. In this case, the counselor is functioning out of her scope of practice. Remember, the client insisted that this treatment methodology be used. The question did not say that the counselor was a trained EMDR practitioner.

147. A: Tarasoff is a landmark case, and if you know no other case, this is the legal case to know. It led to improving services for mental health by requiring mental health practitioners to warn potential victims of imminent harm. We are mandatory reporters. We

must take reasonable steps to protect possible victims from harm. Reasonable steps are those that any person who cares about another person would take to secure that person's safety. Usually that involves informing potential victims and law enforcement agencies.

148. D: Whether said in jest or not, it is the counselor's duty to assess lethality. The counselor needs to assess whether or not the client has a plan and a means to complete the act. The counselor could be held liable if he is negligent in assessing lethality. You have to take seriously any comments made about suicide.

149. C: The APA is the American Psychological Association and is the national organization for psychologists. The ACA is the American Counselors Association and is the national organization for counselors. The NCE, of course, is the National Counselor's Exam. NASP is the National Association for School Psychologists.

150. B: You may have chosen A because he might be an alcoholic. But remember that this section is about professional practices and ethics, so we are talking about an impaired professional. An impaired professional is one who is not able to function in an effective or ethical manner due to a personal problem such as alcohol abuse or other neurological problems. The counselor may be burned out, but the issue is that he is impaired because of his use of alcohol.

151. A: Most ethical guidelines suggest that the best course of action is to confront the impaired professional first and then report him to the licensing board if he continues to come to work impaired.

152. B: If a client comes to you with a problem with which you have very little experience or training, the ethical course of action is to refer the client to someone else who has the proper training and experience. Studying about a particular disorder may help you to better understand the dynamics of the disorder, but it is no substitute for actual training and experience. Treating the man for something that is directly related to the problem he reports is not the standard of professional practice you want to avow.

153. C: An adult student, as the one described in this question, is given the same rights that any adult is given. The student has the right to view his educational records without the consent of his parents, as he is an adult. The Family Educational Rights and Privacy Act affords him the right to have access to his own records. If the student were under the age of 18, parental permission would be required.

154. D: Just as medical doctors are encouraged not to treat family members or friends, so too counselors and mental health professional are discouraged from treating family members or friends. Because the counselor would be treating his cousin, this would be considered a dual relationship. He is a cousin and a therapist. The potential for harm to the client exists and that is why this is considered unethical.

155. C: This is blatantly unethical. The potential for harm to the client exists. This is considered sexual misconduct.

156. D: There are a number of ethical violations in this scenario. The most blatant is requiring your clients to purchase your materials. You seek to profit from the purchase of these materials, which is ethically wrong. Another issue related to this scenario is that your requirements for purchase set up a power differential that should be avoided. You might consider this double-dipping. You get paid by their insurance company to provide treatment and you profit from the sale of your own materials.

157. B: The standards for submission to most professional journals include using APA format. Most scholarly material is written in this form, at least in the mental health field. MLA format is often used in literary journals and comes from the journalism and communications fields.

158. C: In this situation it is appropriate to use a sliding fee scale as the client clearly cannot afford your usual fee. If you were to require him to make installment payments, you would be putting undue burden on him and may cause him emotional and financial harm. You could make a referral to someone else, but the same scenario may present itself there, too. Refusing to see the client unless he can pay your usual fee is a form of abandonment.

159. A: Whenever you are going to begin a therapy group, you must screen all of the possible clients to make sure that they are good candidates for group therapy. You do not need to diagnose each client. Allowing the clients to try the group before committing to it really hampers the group process.

160. B: Clearly this is unethical. This scenario describes a situation in which the counselor profits from the referrals. If the counselor is working for a community agency, most likely he receives a salary for his work. Referring clients to your own private practice has the potential to harm the client and provides you with additional money. An ethical violation of scope of practice would be a scenario in which a counselor lacks appropriate training and supervision to perform or engage in some treatment. In a dual relationship violation, the counselor basically wears multiple hats in the relationship with the client—the therapist and a neighbor or friend.

161. D: Informed consent is the practice of providing the client with all the information so that he or she may agree to or reject treatment, testing, or interventions. Informed consent involves discussing the process of therapy, the limits of confidentiality, possible outcomes of therapy (positive and negative), any risks to the client, and clinic procedures for billing and missed appointments. Informed consent is given in writing.

162. C: Having business cards with "Dr." on them is misrepresentation, since the counselor has not received his doctoral degree. It does not matter that "Professional Counselor" was also on the business card. Clients who see "Dr." usually assume that the person has received a doctorate.

163. D: If a counselor plans to close his practice, he must inform all of his clients of that fact, provide the clients with referrals to other professionals, and notify all clients of the safeguards for the clinical records. If these procedures are not followed, the counselor could be violating ethical standards by abandoning his clients.

164. C: Early. Early remission is no stimulant use criteria being met (except for craving) for at least 3 but less than 12 months. Sustained remission is no stimulant use criteria being met (except for cravings) for 12 months or longer. The terms full and partial are no longer used to describe remission.

165. B: "V" codes are used when what is being treated is not classified as a mental disorder but is the focus of treatment. An example of this would be uncomplicated bereavement. In the DSM coding system, the V replaces the first digit of the five-digit code.

166. A: You should know that Gerald Caplan conceptualized mental health consultation by describing numerous types such as client-centered consultation and consultee-centered consultation. Satir is a well-known family therapist. Adler is a Neo-Freudian theorist. And Holland is associated with career counseling.

167. A: The best course of action is to rectify any misconceptions that your client has about you and your expertise. Along these same lines, anyone she referred to you also needs to be made aware that you are not an expert. Using her story on your website and asking her for a testimonial are unethical. Using unsolicited testimonials is not unethical, but think about the standards of practice that you want associated with your name. Accepting referrals without any explanation puts you in a difficult position, as those who are referred to you may actually believe that you are an expert.

168. C: Sexual misconduct yields the highest number of malpractice cases for all mental health professionals. The other malpractice cases usually focus on breaches of confidentiality.

169. B: PL 94-142 guarantees free and appropriate education for all handicapped children. Another part of this law is that handicapped children are to be placed in the least restrictive educational environment that is most appropriate for a particular child. All handicapped children are to have an individualized educational plan as well. The least restrictive environment is most often in a public school setting.

170. B: It is unethical to accept payment for referrals or to pay someone who referred clients to you. If you want to thank someone for a referral, a thank you note is most appropriate. Offering to buy her lunch on a monthly basis is unethical.

171. C: The DSM system is based on the medical model that looks at client's disease states or mental conditions. None of the other options are appropriate.

172. B: Family therapists look at families as systems, its members as units that interact together and influence each other. Therefore, when choosing the best answer here, you can easily eliminate those answers that talk about families interacting together and influencing one another. The only response that doesn't describe this is B: Usually members of families are unaware of how they influence one another.

173. D: One way that you can think of this is in terms of why couples seek counseling. Usually couples seek counseling because they are not getting along. There is conflict that is unresolved. Families usually don't enter into family therapy because of unresolved conflicts or destructive habits. They usually enter counseling because one member of the family is having problems. Existential and psychodynamic therapies do not address breaking out of destructive habits, although psychodynamic therapy may address unresolved conflicts.

174. B: Panic disorder. Criteria for generalized anxiety disorder specifies excessive worry about a number of events or activities as opposed to an isolated fear or concern. Further, it tends to persist for long periods rather than having an abrupt onset. Somatization disorder is characterized by complaints regarding several organ systems involving different body sites and functions, rather a single body organ. Post-traumatic stress disorder requires confronting an event or events that involve actual or threatened death or serious injury. The client was away at school, did not witness his father's death, and it didn't pose any direct threat to him. Panic attacks involve sudden onset, profound fear of death, and other symptoms such as those the client has described. Common treatment medications: Paxil, Klonopin, Tofranil, Celexa, Librium, Valium, Xanax.

175. B: When diagnosing schizophrenia, there are active and passive symptoms. Active symptoms are exaggerated and passive symptoms are absent. In the daily functioning of persons with schizophrenia, they experience many distortions in their thinking processes and are usually unable or minimally able to address activities of daily living (dressing, preparing meals, etc.).

176. B: The term described in this question is homeostasis. None of the other terms are related to family therapy.

177. A: When a family enters into therapy, each family member must make adjustments, adjust to these changes, and maintain balance. Remember, the family wants to maintain homeostasis (balance), yet the family makes changes to which each family member must adjust and become stable again.

178. A: Triangulation and "enmeshment" are two common terms in family therapy. Yes, the family power structure is out of balance, but what is happening is that some of the family members are forming an unhealthy coalition against another family member. If you visualize this, it is like a triangle. Enmeshment occurs when there is diffusion of boundaries. There are intrusions where none should be made. It is as if one member of the family were trying to live through another member of that family.

179. C: This is an example of enmeshment. Here the mother is trying to dominate or live her life through her daughter. An example of negative attention seeking would be if the daughter constantly misbehaved to get her mother or father to pay attention to her. Disequilibrium refers more to family structure than behaviors. Triangulation is described in the previous question.

180. D: You will need to be familiar with numerous family therapy techniques. One of the more common techniques that a therapist may suggest is time-out. This is the removal of the child from the situation so that all attention is withdrawn from the child. Coercion, by definition, is forcible manipulation of a person to do what you want the person to do. The Premack principle states that more probable behaviors will reinforce less probable behaviors. You use something the child likes to do to get her to do what you want her to do: If she cleans her room, then she can watch TV. Shaping is another behavioral technique that involves successive approximations of a desired behavior being reinforced as a means to teach a desired response.

181. B: This is an example of the Premack principle. Positive reinforcement would occur when a child produces a desired behavior and you provide positive feedback and reinforcement to increase the chances that the child will produce the same behavior again. Negative reinforcement is the taking away of an undesirable consequence to increase the likelihood that the child will engage in the behavior again (you stop nagging if she cleans her room). Quid pro quo is another behavioral technique that essentially means you get something for something: I will do something for you if you do something for me.

182. C: Unlike individual therapy, family therapy believes that one family member's behavior influences all other members' behavior in a circular manner. What one person in the family does affects everyone else. Family members do not act independently of one another. Problems concern everyone, not just one person. The linear model of causality reflects individual therapy. An individual's behavior causes something to occur independent of other factors.

183. B: Bowen's theory is known as family systems theory, and Minuchin's theory is known as structural family theory. Bowen views the family as a system whereby each family member's behavior affects everyone else's behavior. He emphasizes the ways in which individual family members differentiate themselves from one another. Minuchin looks specifically at the structure of the family. He looks at enmeshment and disengagement. Satir's theory is called conjoint family therapy and is involved in communication patterns and meta-communication.

184. D: This is an example of quid pro quo: If you do something for me, I'll do something for you.

185. B: Satir's therapy is known as conjoint family therapy. Strategic family therapy is generally associated with Haley and Madanes. Integrated family therapy involves languaging. Family systems therapy is associated with Bowen.

186. C: Whitaker uses all of the techniques in this question except maximizing languaging, which is incorporated in integrative family therapy. Whitaker believes that it is important to view the family as a unit. So, he helps families set boundaries, develop a sense of who they are as families (family nationalism) and of taking apart and rejoining the family.

187. D: Family therapists are actively involved in the process. They are fairly structured and give homework assignments to families. They are generally flexible and go with the flow of the family. Oftentimes, family therapists "join" with families rather than keeping their distance.

188. D: Haley's strategic family therapy focuses on how families use or abuse power, how they fail to communicate effectively and clearly, and how a symptom serves as a protection against something that is painful.

189. A: A counselor who sees couples for sex therapy must first rule out any physical problems one or the other partner may or may not have. Therefore, one of the first courses of action is to have the couple see their physician to verify that there are no physiological reasons for the dysfunction.

190. B: Sensate focus exercises are used to eliminate performance anxiety by instructing the couple to engage in touching that is nonsexual or nonerotic. The thought here is that if the couple can feel comfortable with touch, then sexual or erotic touch will not be as threatening.

191. D: Blended families are the result of broken relationships. Therefore, when working with blended families, counselors need to address expectations that members of the blended family have about what relationships should be like (based on prior experiences). Counselors also have to assist blended families with the grief associated with losses and help members of the blended family adjust to changes within the family.

192. C: Alfred Adler founded many child guidance clinics and thus is attributed with being one of the first family counselors. Ackerman and Satir would be considered psychoanalytic family therapists, and Rogers would be a family-centered therapist. Another way to think about this question is to look at dates: Adler was around earlier than any of the other three.

193. C: The only logical answer here is C, because Adler did not look at irrational beliefs. He was concerned with feelings of inferiority, social interest, and goals of behavior. Just as with individual therapy, rational-emotive family therapy looks at irrational beliefs.

194. A: Communication patterns generally look at what is said, while meta-communication looks at how something is said.

195. B: You should know that enmeshment and disengagement are concepts in Minuchin's theory of family therapy. Adler looked at goals of behavior, social interest, and overcoming